P9-DXC-403

D0435355

Great Grilling
—— for ——
Friends & Family

Jean Paré

ENTERTAINING & LIFESTYLE

CALGARY PUBLIC LIBRARY

MAY   2015

Copyright © 2014 by Company's Coming Publishing Limited

First printed in 2014   10 9 8 7 6 5 4 3 2 1

Printed in China

All rights reserved worldwide. No part of this book may be reproduced, stored in
a retrieval system or transmitted in any form by any means without written permission
in advance from the publisher.

In the case of photocopying or other reprographic copying, a license may be purchased from
the Canadian Copyright Licensing Agency (Access Copyright). Visit www.accesscopyright.ca
or call toll free 1-800-893-5777. In the United States, please contact the Copyright Clearance
Centre at www.copyright.com or call 978-646-8600.

Brief portions of this book may be reproduced for review purposes, provided credit is given
to the source. Reviewers are invited to contact the publisher for additional information.

Library and Archives Canada Cataloguing in Publication

Paré, Jean, author
Great grilling for friends and family / Jean Paré.
(Entertaining and lifestyle)
Includes index.
ISBN 978-1-77207-000-2 (wire-o)
1. Barbecuing. 2. Cookbooks. I. Title.
TX840.B3P387 2015   641.5'784   C2014-908267-3

Company's Coming Publishing Limited

87 Pender Street East
Vancouver, British Columbia, Canada V6A 1S9
www.companyscoming.com

Company's Coming is a registered trademark owned by Company's Coming
Publishing Limited

We acknowledge the financial support of the Government of Canada through the
Canada Book Fund (CFB) for our publishing activities.

Printed in China

PC: 27

Contents

The Company's Coming Legacy

Jean Paré (pronounced "jeen PAIR-ee") grew up understanding that the combination of family, friends and home cooking is the best recipe for a good life. When Jean left home, she took with her a love of cooking, many family recipes and an intriguing desire to read cookbooks as if they were novels!

"Never share a recipe you wouldn't use yourself."

When her four children had all reached school age, Jean volunteered to cater the 50th anniversary celebration of the Vermilion School of Agriculture, now Lakeland College, in Alberta, Canada. Working out of her home, Jean prepared a dinner for more than 1,000 people, launching a flourishing catering operation that continued for over 18 years.

As requests for her recipes increased, Jean was often asked the question, "Why don't you write a cookbook?" The publication of *150 Delicious Squares* on April 14, 1981 marked the debut of what would soon become one of the world's most popular cookbook series.

Company's Coming cookbooks are distributed in Canada, the United States, Australia and other world markets. Bestsellers many times over in English, Company's Coming cookbooks have also been published in French and Spanish.

Familiar and trusted in home kitchens around the world, Company's Coming cookbooks are offered in a variety of formats. Highly regarded as kitchen workbooks, the softcover Original Series, with its lay-flat plastic comb binding, is still a favourite among readers.

Jean Paré's approach to cooking has always called for *quick and easy recipes* using *everyday ingredients.* That view has served her well.

Jean continues to share what she calls The Golden Rule of Cooking: *Never share a recipe you wouldn't use yourself.* It's an approach that has worked—*millions of times over!*

Foreword

Good company and great food create a powerful combination. When laughter and conversation mix with the heady fragrance and flavours of delicious fare, we are not just sharing a meal—we are nourishing our lives. Artfully prepared dishes awaken the senses and please the palate. And here's the secret: It can be simple!

Casual, fun and delicious—this is the essence of backyard grilling. When the warmth of summer beckons us outside, the last thing we want to do is cook dinner indoors. Grilling takes us not just outside of our kitchens, but beyond the formality of the dining room and into a space where long summer nights encourage us to enjoy the good life with friends and family. And the good life was never so appetizing, or so easy! The flavourful marinades, rubs and infusions in this book make playing with food a grownup affair, while easy cleanup, minimal planning and quick results make grilling especially appealing.

Great Grilling for Friends & Family is designed to help home cooks create sumptuous food without the fuss. It features full-colour photographs of each recipe, preparation tips and tricks, how-to photos, imaginative presentation ideas and helpful information on entertaining, so you and your guests can really savour the food—and your time together.

Great Grilling for Friends & Family opens the door to the backyard and invites you to experience the thrill of the grill. The focus is on the unique flavours and flexibility of grilled food, and the way that cooking on the deck or patio makes for outdoor entertaining at its best. Using seasonal and locally available meats and produce, home chefs can don their

aprons and heat things up—in the lazy days of summer and all year long.

Experiment with the 80 sophisticated but approachable recipes in this book; then treat guests to your favourites. Pull out your patio lanterns and create the perfect atmosphere for connecting with close friends and family.

Great Grilling Basics

The recipes in this book use a number of grilling tools and methods. To ensure fabulous results, familiarize (or reacquaint) yourself with some basic grilling techniques, tips and tools.

GENERAL TIPS FOR SUCCESS

- Prepare the grill:

  - Make sure the grill is clean to start with.

  - Preheat the barbecue. Use a barbecue thermometer to get an accurate reading on the inside to establish and then maintain the right temperature. This is especially important for indirect grilling.

  - Grease the grill well to prevent food from sticking.

- Unless otherwise directed, keep the lid closed at all times. This helps maintain the temperature of the barbecue, reduces risk of flare-ups and reduces cooking time.

- Watch the weather. The temperature outdoors will affect the barbecue's internal temperature. Account for this in cooking times.

- Don't leave the barbecue unattended, especially if there are children nearby.

- Use a meat thermometer to determine meat's doneness. To get an accurate reading, insert the thermometer into the thickest part of the meat.

- When using marinades, always let food marinate in the refrigerator. If you want to use the leftover marinade, always boil it gently for at least five minutes first.

BASIC METHODS

DIRECT GRILLING

This is what most people think of when they think of grilling. Used mainly for small or thin cuts of meat, direct grilling is simply that—cooking the food over the flame or heat source.

Getting ready

For a non-gas barbecue, light coals in a chimney starter and allow them to heat until they begin to turn red. Carefully dump them into the bottom of the barbecue, spreading them in an even layer. For a gas barbecue, simply light the burner or burners over which the food will be cooked.

Barbecue temperatures

For the recipes in *Great Grilling for Friends & Family,* we've referred to levels of heat—low, medium-low, medium, medium-high and high. The following table shows the temperature ranges that correspond with each level of heat:

Level	Barbecue's Internal Temperature
Low	300°F – 350°F (150°C – 175°C)
Medium-low	350°F – 400°F (175°C – 200°C)
Medium	400°F – 450°F (200°C – 230°C)
Medium-high	450°F – 500°F (230°C – 260°C)
High	500°F+ (260°C+)

INDIRECT GRILLING

When you are using your barbecue the same way you would an indoor oven, you're using the indirect grilling method. This method is usually used to cook anything that requires a longer cooking time, such as ribs or roasts. To grill indirectly, place food in the barbecue on a rotisserie, on a rack above the grill or on top of an unlit burner. Indirect cooking's more moderate heat and longer cooking time are also perfect for smoking meat.

Getting ready

For a non-gas barbecue, light coals in a chimney starter and allow them to heat until they begin to turn red. Carefully dump the coals in the portion of the barbecue that will be away from the food you're cooking, either on one side or on two opposite sides. For a gas barbecue, simply light the burner or burners, but cook the food over the burner or burners that are not lit.

Barbecue temperatures

As with direct grilling, we've referred to levels of heat—medium-low, medium and high. The following table shows the temperature ranges that correspond with each level of heat:

Level	Barbecue's Internal Temperature
Medium-low	250°F – 325°F (120°C – 160°C)
Medium	350°F – 400°F (175°C – 200°C)
High	425°F+ (220°C+)

More indirect grilling methods

These methods allow for a lot of variation in how you prepare your food. In *Great Grilling for Friends & Family,* we've experimented with the following indirect grilling methods:

- Rotisserie grilling – This method uses a spit that rotates in the barbecue to allow for slow, even cooking. Be sure to follow the manufacturer's instructions for your particular barbecue rotisserie.

- Smoking – This is a process that infuses the meat with smoky flavours while it is being grilled. Depending on the type of wood chips being used, the meat will pick up different flavour notes from the smoke produced. To smoke meat, place a smoker box filled with pre-soaked wood chips on one burner and turn it on to High. Once smoke begins to form, adjust the burner temperature to achieve the desired internal barbecue temperature. Cook your meat over the unlit burner, according to your recipe. To make your own smoker box, add soaked and drained wood chips to a 7 x 3 inch (18 x 7.5 cm) disposable foil pan. Cover tightly with foil. Poke a few holes in the foil to allow smoke to escape.

Using a drip pan

A drip pan placed underneath indirectly grilled meat will catch any grease or meat juices released while the meat is cooking. To use a drip pan, place it on one burner and light the opposite burner. Place your food on the grill rack that sits over the drip pan.

Spiced Lime Shrimp with Chilled Avocado Soup

Lime-finished shrimp and creamy avocado soup perform in a duet of flavours—enjoy them together to fully appreciate the complex blend of seasonings.

Large avocado, chilled, chopped	1	1
Prepared chicken broth, chilled	1/2 cup	125 mL
Lemon juice	2 tbsp.	30 mL
Granulated sugar	1 tsp.	5 mL
Ground cumin	1 tsp.	5 mL
Salt	1/4 tsp.	1 mL
Whipping cream	1/2 cup	125 mL
Brown sugar, packed	2 tbsp.	30 mL
Tequila	2 tsp.	10 mL
Chili powder	1 tsp.	5 mL
Salt	1/2 tsp.	2 mL
Uncooked large shrimp (peeled and deveined), butterflied (see Tip, below)	1 lb.	454 g
Lime juice	1 tbsp.	15 mL

In a blender or food processor, process first 6 ingredients until smooth. Add cream and process until just combined. Pour into 8 small cups or bowls.

Combine next 4 ingredients. Add shrimp and stir. Cook in greased preheated barbecue wok on direct medium-high heat for about 3 minutes, stirring occasionally, until shrimp turn pink.

Add lime juice and toss. Serve with soup. Serves 8.

---

1 serving: 170 Calories; 10 g Total Fat (4 g Mono, 1 g Poly, 3.5 g Sat); 105 mg Cholesterol; 8 g Carbohydrate (2 g Fibre, 4 g Sugar); 12 g Protein; 350 mg Sodium

TIP
Make this recipe with any size shrimp you happen to have on hand. Adjust cooking times to ensure they are served up tender and juicy.

Paneer Vegetable Kabobs with Mint "Raita"

Madras curry paste provides a pleasing, medium heat to well-spiced vegetables and paneer. Tzatziki sauce with added mint creates a "raita" that provides a soothing contrast to the spices.

Tzatziki sauce	1 cup	250 mL
Chopped mint	3 tbsp.	45 mL
Tomato sauce	1 cup	250 mL
Cooking oil	1 tbsp.	15 mL
Lemon juice	1 tbsp.	15 mL
Liquid honey	1 tbsp.	15 mL
Madras curry paste	1 tbsp.	15 mL
Mango chutney, larger pieces chopped	1 tbsp.	15 mL
Paneer cubes (about 1 inch, 2.5 cm)	8	8
Small Asian eggplant, cut into 8 equal pieces (about 1 inch, 2.5 cm)	1	1
Small red pepper, cut into 16 equal pieces (about 1 inch, 2.5 cm)	1	1
Small zucchini, cut into 8 equal pieces (about 1 inch, 2.5 cm)	1	1
Poultry lacers (see Tip, below)	8	8

Combine tzatziki and mint.

Combine next 6 ingredients in a large resealable freezer bag.

Add next 4 ingredients and chill for 2 hours. Remove paneer and vegetables, reserving marinade.

Thread paneer and vegetables alternately onto lacers. Grill on direct medium heat for about 10 minutes, turning occasionally and brushing with marinade, until vegetables are tender-crisp. Serve with tzatziki mixture. Makes 8 skewers.

---

1 kabob with 1 tbsp. (15 mL) tzatziki mixture: 120 Calories; 7 g Total Fat (1 g Mono, 0.5 g Poly, 5 g Sat); 25 mg Cholesterol; 11 g Carbohydrate (2 g Fibre, 6 g Sugar); 2 g Protein; 460 mg Sodium

TIP
Use poultry lacers instead of wooden picks or skewers, which you have to soak to prevent them from burning on the grill. The metal of the poultry lacers conducts heat, bringing it to the centres of the vegetable and paneer pieces for more even cooking.

Margarita Chicken Cocktails

Start with a pitcher of margaritas on the patio, then bring out these fun chicken appetizers. An elegant, refreshing alternative to a seafood cocktail.

Boneless, skinless chicken thighs	3/4 lb.	340 g
Margarita mix	1/2 cup	125 mL
Cooking oil	2 tbsp.	30 mL
Tequila	2 tbsp.	30 mL
Frozen concentrated orange juice	1 tbsp.	15 mL
Seasoned salt	1 tbsp.	15 mL
Garlic cloves, minced	2	2
Salt	2 tbsp.	30 mL
Lime wedge	1	1
Shredded lettuce, lightly packed	1 cup	250 mL
Avocado slices (1/2 inch, 12 mm, thick)	12	12
Orange juice	1 tbsp.	15 mL

Pound chicken thighs between sheets of plastic wrap until flattened.

Combine next 6 ingredients in a large resealable freezer bag. Add chicken and chill for 1 hour. Drain marinade into a saucepan. Gently boil on medium until reduced by half. Grill chicken on direct medium heat for about 4 minutes per side until no longer pink inside. Let stand until cool enough to handle. Cut into thin strips. Add reduced marinade and toss.

Measure salt onto saucer. Rub lime wedge around rims of 4 cocktail glasses. Press rims into salt to coat. Put lettuce into glasses.

Toss avocado in orange juice and arrange over lettuce. Add chicken. Makes 4 cocktails.

---

1 cocktail: 380 Calories; 25 g Total Fat (15 g Mono, 4.5 g Poly, 3.5 g Sat); 70 mg Cholesterol; 18 g Carbohydrate (7 g Fibre, 9 g Sugar); 19 g Protein; 2400 mg Sodium

ABOUT TEQUILA

This distilled liquor is made from the fermented juice of the Mexican agave plant. To be considered authentic, tequila must be made from agave grown in specific areas of the five Mexican states of Guanajuato, Jalisco, Michoacan de Ocampo, Nayarit and Tamaulipas.

Puffed Pizza Margherita

Classic margherita toppings and zesty pesto cover an innovative pizza crust for an easy, delicious starter. Adventurous chefs may want to try other fast-cooking toppings such as figs and soft goat cheese or pears and Camembert.

Package of puff pastry (14 oz., 397 g), thawed according to package directions	1/2	1/2
Basil pesto	2 tbsp.	30 mL
Bocconcini, thinly sliced	3 oz.	85 g
Seeded chopped Roma (plum) tomatoes	1 cup	250 mL
Chopped fresh basil	2 tbsp.	30 mL
White balsamic vinegar	1 tbsp.	15 mL
Granulated sugar	1/2 tsp.	2 mL

Roll out pastry to a 9 × 9 inch (23 × 23 cm) square. Using a fork, prick holes all over both sides of pastry. Transfer to a baking sheet or 12 inch (30 cm) round pizza pan. Prepare grill for direct high heat. Place pastry on grill and reduce burner under pastry to medium-low, keeping opposite burner on high. Cook for about 7 minutes until pastry is puffed and bottom is golden. Turn pastry over and rotate 180°. Cook for about 7 minutes until golden. Turn off both burners.

Brush pastry with pesto and arrange cheese over top. Close lid and let stand on grill for about 3 minutes until cheese is melted. Remove from grill and cut into 8 pieces.

Toss remaining 4 ingredients together and scatter over pizza. Makes 8 pieces.

---

1 piece: 190 Calories; 13 g Total Fat (5 g Mono, 1 g Poly, 4 g Sat); 5 mg Cholesterol; 13 g Carbohydrate (TRACE Fibre, TRACE Sugar); 5 g Protein; 115 mg Sodium

Tuscan Turkey Rolls

A divine mixture of sun-dried tomatoes, pine nuts, Parmesan cheese and garlic create the stuffing for these beautiful rolls—an aria of texture and flavour! A wash of balsamic vinegar, maple syrup and Dijon adds extra zest.

Turkey scaloppine	3	3
Sun-dried tomato pesto	3 tbsp.	45 mL
Chopped toasted pine nuts (see How To, page 132)	2 tbsp.	30 mL
Grated Parmesan cheese	2 tbsp.	30 mL
Garlic cloves, minced	2	2
Olive oil	1 tbsp.	15 mL
Balsamic vinegar	1/4 cup	60 mL
Olive oil	3 tbsp.	45 mL
Maple syrup	2 tbsp.	30 mL
Dijon mustard	1 tbsp.	15 mL

Pound scaloppine between sheets of plastic wrap to an even thickness. Combine next 5 ingredients and spread over top. Roll up from a long side and secure with wooden picks.

Combine remaining 4 ingredients, reserving 1/4 cup (60 mL). Grill rolls on direct medium heat for about 12 minutes, turning occasionally and brushing with remaining vinegar mixture, until turkey is no longer pink inside. Cover with foil and let stand for 5 minutes. Remove picks and slice diagonally into 4 pieces each. Serve with reserved vinegar mixture. Makes 12 rolls.

1 roll with 1 tbsp (15 ml) vinegar mixture: 110 Calories; 7 g Total Fat (3.5 g Mono, 1 g Poly, 1 g Sat); 0 mg Cholesterol; 4 g Carbohydrate (0 g Fibre, 3 g Sugar); 8 g Protein; 65 mg Sodium

ABOUT PINE NUTS
Pine nuts have a relatively high oil content and burn easily, so take care when toasting them.

MAKE AHEAD
Rolls can be formed and then chilled, covered, until you're ready to grill them. To gain even more breathing room before guests arrive, whip up the vinegar mixture in advance.

Antipasto Kabobs

When food is this fun, it becomes an event. A visit to your favourite Italian deli starts the process. Transforming a familiar assortment into an eye-catching starter on a stick guarantees even more smiles.

Calabrese salami slices	8	8
Bocconcini, halved	8	8
Baguette bread slices (1/4 inch, 6 mm, thick) (see Tip, below)	16	16
Bamboo skewers (4 inches, 10 cm, each), soaked in water for 10 minutes	8	8
Sun-dried tomato and oregano dressing	1/3 cup	75 mL
Finely chopped canned artichoke hearts	2 tbsp.	30 mL
Finely chopped fresh basil	1 tbsp.	15 mL

Thread 1 salami slice and 2 bocconcini halves between 2 baguette slices on each skewer. Grill on direct medium heat for about 2 minutes per side until bread is crisp and cheese is heated through but not melted.

Combine remaining 3 ingredients and drizzle over skewers. Makes 8 kabobs.

1 kabob: 170 Calories; 11 g Total Fat (3 g Mono, 0.5 g Poly, 3.5 g Sat); 20 mg Cholesterol; 10 g Carbohydrate (TRACE Fibre, 1 g Sugar); 8 g Protein; 445 mg Sodium

TIP
Choose a small-diameter, dense baguette that will stay securely on the skewer.

Bourbon Chicken Wings

Your favourite barbecue sauce is given added dimension with the heady richness of bourbon and the satisfying sweetness of orange juice and honey. Guests will happily hover around—and quickly devour—a basket of these tasty wings.

Barbecue sauce	1 cup	250 mL
Bourbon	1/2 cup	125 mL
Frozen concentrated orange juice	1/4 cup	60 mL
Liquid honey	1/4 cup	60 mL
Seasoned salt	1 tsp.	5 mL
Split chicken wings, tips discarded	3 lbs.	1.4 kg

Combine first 5 ingredients, reserving 1/2 cup (125 mL).

Pour remaining barbecue sauce mixture into a large resealable freezer bag. Add chicken wings and chill for 2 hours. Drain and discard marinade. Grill wings on direct medium-low heat for about 15 minutes per side until no longer pink at the bone. Brush with reserved barbecue sauce mixture during final 10 minutes of cooking. Makes 30 to 35 wings.

---

1 wing: *140 Calories; 8 g Total Fat (3 g Mono, 1.5 g Poly, 2 g Sat); 40 mg Cholesterol; 5 g Carbohydrate (0 g Fibre, 3 g Sugar); 9 g Protein; 180 mg Sodium*

EXPERIMENT!

Try for different shades of flavour by using a smoky barbecue sauce one time and a hot and spicy one the next.

Shrimp and Pineapple Citrus Skewers

Tropical flavours set the stage for your own backyard luau. The bright citrus notes, gingery heat and fresh cilantro give the shrimp and pineapple their party-style punch.

Orange juice	1/2 cup	125 mL
Brown sugar, packed	3 tbsp.	45 mL
Finely grated ginger root	1 tbsp.	15 mL
Salt	1/2 tsp.	2 mL
Pepper	1/2 tsp.	2 mL
Uncooked extra-large shrimp (peeled and deveined)	20	20
Grated orange zest	1/2 tsp.	2 mL
Pineapple pieces (1 inch, 2.5 cm, each)	20	20
Bamboo skewers (4 inches, 10 cm, each), soaked in water for 10 minutes	20	20
Chopped fresh cilantro	1 tbsp.	15 mL

Combine first 5 ingredients in a large resealable freezer bag. Add shrimp and chill for 30 minutes. Drain marinade into a saucepan. Simmer on medium-low until reduced by half. Stir in orange zest.

Thread 1 pineapple piece and 1 shrimp onto each skewer. Grill on direct medium heat for about 3 minutes per side, brushing often with reduced marinade, until shrimp turn pink.

Sprinkle with cilantro. Makes 20 skewers.

1 skewer: 40 Calories; 0 g Total Fat (0 g Mono, 0 g Poly, 0 g Sat); 35 mg Cholesterol; 4 g Carbohydrate (0 g Fibre, 3 g Sugar); 5 g Protein; 95 mg Sodium

ABOUT SHRIMP

Shrimp are sold according to size, but keep in mind that the perception of size varies from region to region, as well as between fish markets. As a general guideline, these are the number of shrimp you can expect to get from a 1 lb. (454 g) measure:

- Jumbo: 11 – 15
- Extra-large: 16 – 20
- Large: 21 – 30
- Medium: 31 – 35
- Small: 36 – 45
- Baby: about 100

Lemon Grass Beef Salad

A plate full of textures and tastes—what a feast! The tang of lime juice, the subtle chili heat and the soothing coolness of orange peppers are just some of the delights that await you.

Lemon grass stalks (bulbs only), finely chopped	2	2
Brown sugar, packed	1/4 cup	60 mL
Lime juice	1/4 cup	60 mL
Soy sauce	3 tbsp.	45 mL
Sesame oil	1 tbsp.	15 mL
Grated lime zest	1 tsp.	5 mL
Chili paste (sambal oelek)	1/2 tsp.	2 mL
Pepper	1/2 tsp.	2 mL
Cooked rice stick noodles (see Tip, below)	4 cups	1 L
Sugar snap peas, trimmed and sliced diagonally	2 cups	500 mL
Slivered orange pepper	1 1/2 cups	375 mL
Chopped fresh cilantro	1/4 cup	60 mL
Chopped fresh mint	1/4 cup	60 mL
Beef strip loin steak	1 lb.	454 g
Salt	1/2 tsp.	2 mL
Pepper	1/4 tsp.	1 mL

Whisk first 8 ingredients together until brown sugar is dissolved.

Combine next 5 ingredients in a large bowl and add 1/2 cup (125 mL) lemon grass mixture. Toss until coated.

Sprinkle steak with salt and pepper. Grill on direct medium-high heat for about 7 minutes per side for medium-rare or until steak reaches desired doneness. Cover with foil and let stand for 10 minutes. Cut diagonally, across the grain, into thin slices and toss with remaining lemon grass mixture. Divide noodle mixture onto 4 serving plates, arranging beef slices over top. Serves 4.

---

1 serving: 570 Calories; 11 g Total Fat (4 g Mono, 1.5 g Poly, 3 g Sat); 55 mg Cholesterol; 85 g Carbohydrate (4 g Fibre, 17 g Sugar); 34 g Protein; 1180 mg Sodium

TIP
To prepare rice noodles, pour boiling water over noodles in a bowl and let stand, covered, for 20 minutes until tender.

Grilled Chicken and Squash on Spinach Salad

It's never too late in the year to take advantage of the natural sweetness elicited from grilled butternut squash. Enjoy this rich harvest of colourful, flavourful delights!

Boneless, skinless chicken thighs (about 6)	1 1/4 lbs.	560 g
Butternut squash, cut into 1/2 inch (12 mm) slices	1 lb.	454 g
Cooking oil	2 tbsp.	30 mL
Granulated sugar	1 tbsp.	15 mL
Ground cinnamon	1 tbsp.	15 mL
Salt	1 tsp.	5 mL
Pepper	1/4 tsp.	1 mL
Baby spinach leaves, lightly packed	8 cups	2 L
Coarsely chopped walnuts, toasted (see How To, page 132)	1/2 cup	125 mL
Thinly sliced red onion	1/2 cup	125 mL
Goat (chèvre) cheese, cut up	2 oz.	57 g
Orange juice	2/3 cup	150 mL
Cooking oil	2 tbsp.	30 mL
Dijon mustard (with whole seeds)	2 tbsp.	30 mL
Brown sugar, packed	1 tbsp.	15 mL

Brush chicken and squash with cooking oil.

Combine next 4 ingredients and sprinkle over top. Grill on direct medium heat for about 5 minutes per side until chicken is no longer pink inside and squash is tender. Let stand until cool enough to handle. Slice chicken into thin strips and cut squash into cubes. Transfer to a large bowl.

Add next 4 ingredients and toss.

Whisk remaining 4 ingredients together until sugar is dissolved. Drizzle over salad and toss. Makes about 10 cups (2.5 L). Serves 4.

---

1 serving: 560 Calories; 34 g Total Fat (13 g Mono, 13 g Poly, 6 g Sat); 125 mg Cholesterol; 32 g Carbohydrate (5 g Fibre, 10 g Sugar); 35 g Protein; 920 mg Sodium

ABOUT SQUASH

The many varieties of squash are divided into two broad categories: summer and winter. The winter varieties, such as butternut squash, are available year-round, but are tastiest from early fall through winter. Winter squash, with its thicker skin, is heartier and has firmer flesh—perfect for grilling.

Lobster, Fennel and Pear Salad

Fruits of the sea and the tree come together in this elegant, aromatic salad. A simple Dijon vinaigrette lets the main attractions, lobster and pear, shine.

Frozen concentrated pineapple juice, thawed	1 cup	250 mL
Liquid honey	6 tbsp.	90 mL
White wine vinegar	6 tbsp.	90 mL
Dijon mustard	2 tbsp.	30 mL
Salt	1 tsp.	5 mL
Pepper	1/2 tsp.	2 mL
Medium fennel bulbs (white part only), thinly sliced	2	2
Lobster tails, halved lengthwise	4	4
Firm medium unpeeled pears, cored and halved	2	2
Spring mix lettuce, lightly packed	4 cups	1 L

Whisk first 6 ingredients together until smooth.

Put fennel into a large bowl. Add half of pineapple juice mixture and toss until coated. Let stand, covered, for 30 minutes.

Grill lobster on direct medium heat for about 4 minutes per side until meat is opaque. Grill pears, cut-side down, for about 2 minutes until grill marks appear.

Add lettuce to fennel mixture and toss. Arrange on a large serving plate. Remove lobster meat from shells and cut into bite-sized pieces. Arrange over lettuce mixture. Cut pear halves into 3 pieces each and arrange around outside edge of plate. Drizzle with remaining pineapple juice mixture. Serves 4.

---

1 serving: *360 Calories; 1 g Total Fat (0 g Mono, 0 g Poly, 0 g Sat); 55 mg Cholesterol; 78 g Carbohydrate (7 g Fibre, 58 g Sugar); 15 g Protein; 940 mg Sodium*

ABOUT LOBSTER TAILS

Usually purchased frozen, lobster tails should be thawed for between eight and ten hours in the refrigerator. They should be kept very cold until they are ready to be used. Once thawed or if purchased fresh, lobster should always be cooked the same day.

Romano Ciabatta Vegetable Salad

The smoky sweetness of grilled vegetables is enhanced by a roasted garlic and balsamic vinaigrette. This salad is a tasty vegetarian meal that everyone at the table will enjoy.

Large fennel bulbs (white part only), cut into 4 wedges each	2	2
Large red onion, cut into 4 wedges (see Tip, below)	1	1
Large eggplant, cut into 3/4 inch (2 cm) slices	1	1
Medium zucchini, quartered lengthwise	2	2
Large red pepper, halved	1	1
Large yellow pepper, halved	1	1
Extra-virgin olive oil	1/4 cup	60 mL
Multigrain ciabatta buns, split	2	2
Can of romano beans, rinsed and drained	19 oz.	540 mL
Grape tomatoes	2 cups	500 mL
Roasted garlic cloves, mashed (see How To, page 152)	4	4
Balsamic vinegar	2/3 cup	150 mL
Extra-virgin olive oil	2/3 cup	150 mL
Granulated sugar	2 tsp.	10 mL
Salt	1/2 tsp.	2 mL
Pepper	1/2 tsp.	2 mL

Brush first 6 ingredients with olive oil. Grill fennel and onion on direct medium heat for about 25 minutes, turning occasionally, until tender. Grill eggplant, zucchini and peppers for about 15 minutes, turning occasionally, until tender-crisp and browned. Let stand until cool enough to handle. Cut fennel and onion into 1 inch (2.5 cm) pieces. Cut eggplant, zucchini and peppers into 1/2 inch (3.8 cm) pieces.

Brush bun halves with olive oil. Grill for 1 to 2 minutes until toasted. Cut into 1 inch (2.5 cm) pieces.

Combine beans and tomatoes with vegetables and bread cubes in a large bowl.

Combine remaining 6 ingredients. Drizzle over salad and toss until coated. Makes about 12 cups (3 L). Serves 6.

---

1 serving: 540 Calories; 36 g Total Fat (27 g Mono, 3 g Poly, 5 g Sat); 0 mg Cholesterol; 52 g Carbohydrate (11 g Fibre, 13 g Sugar); 10 g Protein; 290 mg Sodium

TIP

Quartering the onion with the stem still on helps the pieces stay intact during grilling. The core of the fennel serves the same stabilizing purpose.

Farmers' Market Pork Tenderloin Salad

A Saturday morning sampling the wares of your local farmers' market acts as the appetizer for this scrumptious salad—chock full of pretty vegetables and tender pork.

Redcurrant jelly, warmed	2 tbsp.	30 mL
Barbecue sauce	1 tbsp.	15 mL
Garlic clove, minced	1	1
Pork tenderloin, trimmed of fat	1 lb.	454 g
Smoked sweet paprika	2 tsp.	10 mL
Large corncobs, in husk, soaked in water for 1 hour, halved crosswise	3	3
Small zucchini, quartered lengthwise	2	2
Large red pepper, quartered	1	1
Cherry tomatoes	16	16
Fresh ground pepper, sprinkle		
Apple cider vinegar	3 tbsp.	50 mL
Redcurrant jelly, warmed	3 tbsp.	50 mL
Olive oil	2 tbsp.	30 mL
Chopped fresh oregano	1 tbsp.	15 mL
Garlic clove, minced	1	1
Salt	1/4 tsp.	1 mL

Combine first 3 ingredients.

Rub tenderloin with paprika. Grill on direct medium heat for about 30 minutes, turning occasionally and brushing with jelly mixture during final 10 minutes of cooking, until internal temperature reaches 155°F (58°C). Cover with foil and let stand for 10 minutes. Cut into thin slices.

Grill next 3 ingredients on direct medium heat for about 30 minutes, turning occasionally, until browned and tender. Let stand until cool enough to handle. Cut corn cobs into 1 inch (2.5 cm) pieces. Cut zucchini and red pepper into 1/2 inch (12 mm) pieces. Transfer to a bowl and add tomatoes and pepper.

Whisk remaining 6 ingredients together until smooth. Drizzle over vegetables and toss until coated. Transfer to a large serving plate, arranging pork slices over top. Serves 4.

---

1 serving: 380 Calories; 14 g Total Fat (9 g Mono, 2 g Poly, 3.5 g Sat); 75 mg Cholesterol; 39 g Carbohydrate (5 g Fibre, 22 g Sugar); 27 g Protein; 290 mg Sodium

Tandoori Paneer Salad

While many of us won't have access to a tandoor, the clay oven that is so essential to the Indian barbecue, the tandoori curry paste in this recipe evokes those exotic flavours.

Tandoori curry paste	3 tbsp.	45 mL
Cooking oil	1 tbsp.	15 mL
Lime juice	1 tbsp.	15 mL
Salt	1 tsp.	5 mL
Cubed paneer (about 1/2 inch, 12 mm, pieces)	3 cups	750 mL
Chopped zucchini (about 1/2 inch, 12 mm, pieces)	2 cups	500 mL
Grape tomatoes	2 cups	500 mL
Chopped onion (about 1/2 inch, 12 mm, pieces)	1 cup	250 mL
Cooking oil	2 tbsp.	30 mL
Brown sugar, packed	1 tbsp.	15 mL
Lime juice	1 tbsp.	15 mL
Salt	1/2 tsp.	2 mL
Baby spinach leaves, lightly packed	6 cups	1.5 L
Cooked brown basmati rice (see Tip, below)	2 cups	500 mL

Combine first 4 ingredients in a large bowl.

Add next 4 ingredients and toss until coated. Cook paneer mixture in a preheated grill wok on direct medium-high heat, stirring occasionally, for about 15 minutes until vegetables are tender-crisp.

Whisk next 4 ingredients until sugar and salt are dissolved. Add spinach and rice, and toss until coated. Divide among 4 serving plates and top with paneer mixture. Serves 4.

---

1 serving: 500 Calories; 25 g Total Fat (6 g Mono, 3 g Poly, 10 g Sat); 45 mg Cholesterol; 53 g Carbohydrate (6 g Fibre, 12 g Sugar); 19 g Protein; 1370 mg Sodium

TIP
Brown basmati rice adds a lovely nutty flavour to this dish, but white basmati works just as well.

Chipotle Chicken Burgers with Avocado Mayonnaise

A creamy avocado sauce cools down the fruity spiciness of the chipotle tomato sauce on these easy chicken burgers. Add a salad and a bottle of your favourite white wine for a relaxing get-together.

Chopped tomato	1 1/2 cups	375 mL
Dark raisins	1/4 cup	60 mL
Frozen concentrated orange juice	2 tbsp.	30 mL
Brown sugar, packed	2 tsp.	10 mL
Finely chopped chipotle pepper in adobo sauce (see Tip, below)	2 tsp.	10 mL
Garlic clove	1	1
Salt	1/2 tsp.	2 mL
Ground cumin	1/4 tsp.	1 mL
Boneless, skinless chicken breast halves (4 – 6 oz., 113 – 170 g, each), pounded to 1/4 inch (6 mm) thickness	4	4
Medium avocado, mashed	1	1
Mayonnaise	2 tbsp.	30 mL
Finely chopped green onion	1 tbsp.	15 mL
Lime juice	2 tsp.	10 mL
Triangular ciabatta buns, split	4	4

In a blender or a food processor, process first 8 ingredients until smooth. Transfer to a large resealable freezer bag and add chicken. Chill for at least 6 hours or overnight. Drain marinade into a saucepan. Gently boil on medium until thickened. Grill chicken on direct medium heat for about 10 minutes, turning often and brushing with thickened marinade, until chicken is no longer pink inside.

Combine next 4 ingredients.

Serve chicken, over a layer of avocado mixture, in buns. Makes 4 burgers.

---

1 burger: 490 Calories; 18 g Total Fat (9 g Mono, 3 g Poly, 2.5 g Sat); 85 mg Cholesterol; 48 g Carbohydrate (6 g Fibre, 15 g Sugar); 40 g Protein; 520 mg Sodium

TIP
Wear rubber gloves when handling chipotle peppers and avoid touching your eyes—and always wash your hands well afterwards. Store any leftover chipotle peppers in an airtight container in the fridge.

Drunken Lamb Burgers with Cranberry Dijon Mustard

Lamb makes a splash in a bath of beer, creating a moist, hearty patty for an intriguing cranberry mustard. Use the condiment with other grilled meats for a fresh new taste.

Fine dry bread crumbs	1/4 cup	60 mL
Finely chopped onion	1/4 cup	60 mL
Tomato paste (see Tip, page 148)	2 tbsp.	30 mL
Chopped fresh rosemary	2 tsp.	10 mL
Garlic cloves, minced	2	2
Salt	1/2 tsp.	2 mL
Ground allspice	1/4 tsp.	1 mL
Lean ground lamb	1 lb.	454 g
Dark or amber ale	1 cup	250 mL
Jellied cranberry sauce	1/2 cup	125 mL
Dijon mustard (with whole seeds)	1/4 cup	60 mL
Brown sugar, packed	2 tbsp.	30 mL
Buns, split	4	4

Combine first 8 ingredients and divide into 4 portions. Shape portions into patties, about 4 inches (10 cm) in diameter. Place patties in a shallow baking dish and add ale. Chill, covered, for at least 6 hours or overnight. Drain and discard marinade. Grill patties on direct medium heat for about 7 minutes per side until internal temperature reaches 160°F (71°C).

Whisk next 3 ingredients together until smooth. Makes about 2/3 cup (150 mL).

Serve patties, on top of about 1 tbsp. (15 mL) cranberry mustard mixture, in buns. The remaining mustard mixture can be stored in the refrigerator for up to 1 week. Makes 4 burgers.

1 burger: 500 Calories; 20 g Total Fat (0 g Mono, 1 g Poly, 11 g Sat); 85 mg Cholesterol; 55 g Carbohydrate (2 g Fibre, 24 g Sugar); 25 g Protein; 870 mg Sodium

ABOUT GROUND LAMB

If you have any trouble finding ground lamb, ask your butcher to grind some fresh for you. Ground lamb can be stored in the refrigerator for up to three days and in the freezer for up to three months.

Sassy Stuffed Portobello Burgers

With jalapeño and chili oil supplying the "sass," this vegetarian burger will please those who prefer to walk on the spicy side of life.

Prepared vegetable broth	2/3 cup	150 mL
Bulgur	1/3 cup	75 mL
Grated jalapeño Monterey Jack cheese	1 cup	250 mL
Salsa	2 tbsp.	30 mL
Ground cumin	1 tsp.	5 mL
Chili oil	1 tbsp.	15 mL
Salt	1/2 tsp.	2 mL
Portobello mushrooms (about 6 oz.,170 g, each), stems and gills removed (see Tip, below)	4	4
Grated jalapeño Monterey Jack cheese	1 cup	250 mL
Mixed baby greens, lightly packed	2 cups	500 mL
Onion buns, split and toasted	2	2
Salsa	1/2 cup	125 mL
Diced avocado	1 cup	250 mL

Bring broth to a boil in a saucepan. Add bulgur and remove from heat. Let stand, covered, for 30 minutes.

Stir in next 3 ingredients.

Combine chili oil and salt. Brush over both sides of mushrooms. Grill, stem-side down, on direct medium-high heat for 5 minutes. Turn and fill portobellos with bulgur mixture.

Sprinkle with second amount of cheese. Cook for about 6 minutes until heated through and cheese is melted.

Arrange greens over bun halves, topping each with 1 stuffed mushroom, salsa and avocado. Makes 4 burgers.

---

1 burger: 450 Calories; 27 g Total Fat (4.5 g Mono, 1 g Poly, 11 g Sat); 60 mg Cholesterol; 35 g Carbohydrate (6 g Fibre, 5 g Sugar); 22 g Protein; 1100 mg Sodium

TIP
Because the gills of the portobellos can sometimes be bitter, be sure to remove them before grilling. First, remove the stems. Then, using a small spoon, scrape out and discard the mushroom gills.

Lemon Grass Crab Cakes with Asparagus

Here's an upscale dish with serious attitude, from its crabmeat patty seasoned with lemon grass and ginger root, to its asparagus bed and puff pastry shell.

Package of puff pastry (14 oz., 397 g), thawed according to package directions	1/2	1/2
Large egg, fork-beaten	1	1
Cans of crabmeat (4 1/4 oz., 120 g, each), drained and cartilage removed, flaked	2	2
Roasted garlic mayonnaise	1/3 cup	75 mL
Panko crumbs	1/4 cup	60 mL
Chopped fresh parsley	2 tbsp.	30 mL
Finely chopped lemon grass (bulb only)	1 tbsp.	15 mL
Finely grated ginger root	2 tsp.	10 mL
Fresh asparagus spears, trimmed of tough ends	16	16
Roasted garlic mayonnaise	1 tbsp.	15 mL

Roll out pastry to a 12 × 10 inch (30 × 25 cm) rectangle. Cut rectangle into 8 smaller rectangles, about 5 × 3 inches (12.5 × 7.5 cm) each. Arrange on a baking sheet and chill, covered, for about 30 minutes.

Brush pastry with egg, then prick with a fork. Bake in a 400°F (200°C) oven for about 15 minutes until golden. Split pastries in half horizontally.

Combine next 6 ingredients and divide into 16 portions. Shape portions into patties, about 1 1/2 inches (3.8 cm) in diameter. Place patties on a sheet of greased heavy-duty (or double layer of regular) foil. Cook on direct medium heat for about 10 minutes per side until golden.

Grill asparagus on direct medium heat for about 5 minutes, turning occasionally, until tender-crisp. Brush asparagus with second amount of mayonnaise during final minute of cooking. Brush any remaining mayonnaise on bottom halves of pastries. Top each with 2 asparagus spears and 2 crab cakes. Place pastry tops over crab cakes. Serves 8.

1 serving: 250 Calories; 17 g Total Fat (9 g Mono, 3.5 g Poly, 3.5 g Sat); 55 mg Cholesterol; 14 g Carbohydrate (1 g Fibre, TRACE Sugar); 10 g Protein; 240 mg Sodium

ABOUT PANKO CRUMBS
Usually used to coat Japanese fried foods, panko crumbs tend to be coarser than regular bread crumbs and can be used the same way.

Greek Pita Burgers

Invite your guests to imagine themselves on a Greek island, taking in the last of the day's rays as they linger over a meal featuring these delicious patties.

Crumbled feta cheese	1/4 cup	60 mL
Fine dry bread crumbs	1/4 cup	60 mL
Finely chopped black olives	1/4 cup	60 mL
Dried oregano	1 tsp.	5 mL
Grated lemon zest	1 tsp.	5 mL
Garlic clove, minced	1	1
Salt	1/2 tsp.	2 mL
Lean ground beef	1 lb.	454 g
Roasted red pepper hummus	1/2 cup	125 mL
Pita breads (7 inch, 18 cm, diameter), warmed (see Tip, below)	4	4
Spinach leaves (stems removed), lightly packed	1 cup	250 mL

Combine first 8 ingredients and divide into 4 portions. Shape portions into half moon-shaped patties. Grill on direct medium heat for about 9 minutes per side until internal temperature reaches 160°F (71°C).

Spread hummus over pitas, arranging spinach over half of each pita. Place patties over spinach and fold pitas in half to enclose. Makes 4 burgers.

---

1 burger: 520 Calories; 22 g Total Fat (10 g Mono, 1.5 g Poly, 8 g Sat); 75 mg Cholesterol; 39 g Carbohydrate (3 g Fibre, 3 g Sugar); 31 g Protein; 770 mg Sodium

TIP

To warm the pita breads, wrap in foil and place on upper rack of barbecue or directly on the grill. Remove when just heated through.

Curry Salmon Burgers with Mango Chutney Mayo

Mango chutney mayonnaise tempers the punch of chili heat in these salmon burgers. The curry can warm you on a winter night, or provide a fine counterpoint to a cold beer on a summer evening.

Mayonnaise	1/3 cup	75 mL
Mango chutney, chopped	1/4 cup	60 mL
Salmon fillet, skin removed and cut into large chunks	1 1/2 lbs.	680 g
Plain yogurt	2 tbsp.	30 mL
Hot curry paste	4 tsp.	20 mL
Fine dry bread crumbs	3/4 cup	175 mL
Chopped fresh cilantro	1/4 cup	60 mL
Chopped green onion	1/4 cup	60 mL
Seasoned salt	1 tsp.	5 mL
Kaiser rolls, split	6	6

Combine mayonnaise and chutney. Chill.

In a blender or food processor, process next 3 ingredients until salmon is coarsely ground. Transfer to a bowl.

Add next 4 ingredients. Mix well and divide into 6 portions. Shape portions into patties, about 4 inches (10 cm) in diameter. Chill, covered, for 2 hours (see Why To, below). Place patties on a sheet of greased heavy-duty (or double layer of regular) foil. Cook on direct medium heat for about 7 minutes per side until internal temperature reaches 160°F (71°C).

Serve patties, topped with mayonnaise mixture, in rolls. Makes 6 burgers.

---

1 burger: 510 Calories; 19 g Total Fat (8 g Mono, 6 g Poly, 3 g Sat); 65 mg Cholesterol; 47 g Carbohydrate (4 g Fibre, 10 g Sugar); 32 g Protein; 1100 mg Sodium

WHY TO
Chilling the uncooked patties before grilling them helps them to hold together.

Blue Cheese Beer Burgers

Perfect for a pre-game party or a post-game get-together, these hearty burgers hold a hint of the beer you can serve with the meal. The Stilton adds a pleasing, creamy sharpness.

Finely chopped onion	1 cup	250 mL
Fine dry bread crumbs	1/2 cup	125 mL
Stout beer	1/3 cup	75 mL
Celery salt	1 tsp.	5 mL
Garlic powder	1 tsp.	5 mL
Pepper	1/2 tsp.	2 mL
Lean ground beef	2 lbs.	900 g
Stilton cheese, sliced	6 oz.	170 g
Onion buns, split	8	8

Combine first 7 ingredients and divide into 8 portions. Shape portions into patties, about 4 inches (10 cm) in diameter. Chill, covered, for 1 hour. Grill patties on direct medium heat for about 5 minutes per side until internal temperature reaches 160°F (71°C). Top with cheese during final minute of cooking.

Serve patties in buns. Makes 8 burgers.

---

1 burger: 530 Calories; 25 g Total Fat (9 g Mono, 0.5 g Poly, 11 g Sat); 85 mg Cholesterol; 36 g Carbohydrate (2 g Fibre, 4 g Sugar); 34 g Protein; 940 mg Sodium

MAKE AHEAD

Patties can be made up to six hours in advance.

EXPERIMENT!

Play up the burgers to your liking by adding various garnishes such as pickled or roasted beets and tomato.

Spicy Asian Patties with Pear Salsa

Sambal oelek gives these pork-and-shrimp patties a spicy kick, while the accompanying Asian pear salsa, exquisitely balanced on a sweet/sour tightrope, cools everything down.

Diced Asian pears	2 cups	500 mL
Diced English cucumber	1 cup	250 mL
Mirin	1/4 cup	60 mL
Finely diced red pepper	2 tbsp.	30 mL
Rice wine vinegar	2 tbsp.	30 mL
Salt	1/8 tsp.	0.5 mL
Pepper	1/8 tsp.	0.5 mL
Chopped fresh cilantro	1/4 cup	60 mL
Soy sauce	2 tbsp.	30 mL
Finely grated ginger root	1 tbsp.	15 mL
Chili paste (sambal oelek)	2 tsp.	10 mL
Garlic powder	1 tsp.	5 mL
Pepper	1/2 tsp.	2 mL
Lean ground pork	1 1/2 lbs.	680 g
Uncooked shrimp (peeled and deveined), finely chopped	1/2 lb.	225 g
Square panini breads (8 × 8 inches, 20 × 20 cm, each)	2	2
Sesame oil	1 tbsp.	15 mL

Combine first 7 ingredients and chill, covered, for at least 1 hour to blend flavours.

Combine next 8 ingredients and divide into 6 portions. Shape portions into patties, about 3/4 inch (2 cm) thick. Chill, covered, for 1 hour. Grill patties on direct medium-high heat for about 6 minutes per side until internal temperature reaches 160°F (71°C).

Brush panini breads with sesame oil. Grill, turning occasionally, until warmed through. Cut each bread into 4 squares, discarding 2 squares. Top remaining squares with patties and serve with pear salsa. Serves 6.

1 serving: 530 Calories; 31 g Total Fat (12 g Mono, 3.5 g Poly, 10 g Sat); 140 mg Cholesterol; 34 g Carbohydrate (2 g Fibre, 11 g Sugar); 32 g Protein; 770 mg Sodium

MAKE AHEAD
The pear salsa can be made a day in advance.

Tuna Squares with Wasabi Ginger Slaw

A glamorous version of the traditional tuna sandwich, this gourmet adaptation is for grownups. Grilled, sesame-flavoured tuna lies on a bed of suey choy slaw spiced up with wasabi and pickled ginger.

Mayonnaise	1/4 cup	60 mL
Wasabi paste	1 tsp.	5 mL
Finely chopped pickled ginger	1 tbsp.	15 mL
Shredded suey choy	1 2/3 cups	400 mL
Sesame oil	1 tbsp.	15 mL
Soy sauce	1 tbsp.	15 mL
Pepper	1/2 tsp.	2 mL
Tuna steaks (about 1 inch, 2.5 cm, thick)	1 lb.	454 g
Square panini bread (8 × 8 inches, 20 × 20 cm)	1	1
Sesame oil	2 tsp.	10 mL

Whisk mayonnaise and wasabi until smooth. Stir in ginger. Add suey choy and toss until combined.

Combine next 3 ingredients in a large resealable freezer bag. Add tuna and chill for 1 hour. Drain and discard marinade. Grill tuna on direct medium-high heat for about 4 minutes per side until medium-rare (see Tip, below). Cut into 8 pieces.

Brush panini bread with sesame oil. Grill, turning occasionally, until warmed through. Cut bread into 9 squares, discarding 1 square. Top remaining squares with suey choy mixture and tuna. Makes 8 squares.

---

1 square: 210 Calories; 12 g Total Fat (5 g Mono, 3.5 g Poly, 1.5 g Sat); 25 mg Cholesterol; 9 g Carbohydrate (TRACE Fibre, TRACE Sugar); 15 g Protein; 290 mg Sodium

TIP
Tuna should be served rare or, at the most, medium-rare. It will become too dry if overcooked.

Brown Rice Veggie Patties with Tomato Relish

Burger lovers who shy away from soy will love this vegetarian version. Brown rice and lentils form the base of this tasty patty, topped with a lively relish.

Large Roma (plum) tomatoes, diced	4	4
Finely chopped sweet onion	1/2 cup	125 mL
Balsamic vinegar	1/4 cup	60 mL
Chopped fresh basil	1/4 cup	60 mL
Extra-virgin olive oil	2 tbsp.	30 mL
Liquid honey	2 tsp.	10 mL
Dried crushed chilies	1/2 tsp.	2 mL
Salt	1/4 tsp.	1 mL
Olive oil	2 tsp.	10 mL
Chopped fresh brown mushrooms	2 cups	500 mL
Chopped sweet onion	1 cup	250 mL
Garlic cloves, minced	2	2
Finely chopped red pepper	1 cup	250 mL
Canned lentils, rinsed and drained	1 1/2 cups	375 mL
Large egg, fork-beaten	1	1
Cooked brown rice	1 1/2 cups	375 mL
Fine dry bread crumbs	1/4 cup	60 mL
Montreal steak spice	2 tsp.	10 mL
Pumpernickel cocktail bread slices	12	12

Combine first 8 ingredients and let stand, covered, for at least 1 hour to blend flavours.

Heat olive oil in a large frying pan on medium-high. Add next 3 ingredients and cook for about 5 minutes, stirring often, until mushrooms are browned.

Add red pepper and cook for about 3 minutes until tender-crisp and liquid is evaporated. Transfer to food processor.

Add lentils and process with on/off motion until lentils are mashed but not puréed. Transfer to a bowl.

Stir in remaining 4 ingredients and divide into 12 portions. Shape portions into patties, about 2 1/2 inches (6.4 cm) in diameter. Grill on direct medium-high heat for about 5 minutes per side until heated through.

(continued on next page)

Top each bread slice with 1 patty. Drain liquid from tomato mixture. Spoon tomato mixture over patties. Makes 12 veggie patties.

1 veggie patty: 190 Calories; 5 g Total Fat (3 g Mono, 1 g Poly, 1 g Sat); 20 mg Cholesterol; 48 g Carbohydrate (4 g Fibre, 4 g Sugar); 7 g Protein; 470 mg Sodium

MAKE AHEAD
The patties can be made up to one day ahead.

Out-of-the-Park Jalapeño Dawgs

A grand-slam dawg like this one needs a big bun and even bigger napkins. Serve this crowd-pleaser with an icy cold pitcher of lemonade or beer and wait for the applause.

Green jalapeño jelly	3 tbsp.	45 mL
Mayonnaise	3 tbsp.	45 mL
Finely chopped pickled jalapeño peppers	1 tbsp.	15 mL
Grated lime zest	1/4 tsp.	1 mL
Green jalapeño jelly	2 tbsp.	30 mL
Lime juice	1 tbsp.	15 mL
Cooking oil	2 tsp.	10 mL
Minced pickled jalapeño peppers	2 tsp.	10 mL
Precooked turkey bratwurst sausages (about 4 oz., 113 g, each)	4	4
Large yellow pepper, quartered	1	1
Red onion slice, about 1/2 inch (12 mm) thick	1	1
Large hoagie buns, partially split	4	4

Combine first 4 ingredients. Set aside.

Combine next 4 ingredients in a separate bowl.

Make diagonal slashes on both sides of sausages (see Why To, below). Grill sausages, yellow pepper and onion slices on direct medium heat for about 15 minutes, turning occasionally and brushing with lime juice mixture, until hot and vegetables are tender-crisp. Chop onion and slice yellow pepper into slivers.

Spread buns with mayonnaise mixture. Serve sausages, topped with onion and yellow pepper, in buns. Makes 4 dawgs.

---

1 dawg: 650 Calories; 39 g Total Fat (21 g Mono, 5 g Poly, 11 g Sat); 115 mg Cholesterol; 41 g Carbohydrate (2 g Fibre, 15 g Sugar); 34 g Protein; 1390 mg Sodium

WHY TO
Cutting into the sausage allows it to cook through to the centre faster and keeps it from curling.

Herbed Turkey Burgers with Fresh Tomato Ketchup

The feta imparts fabulous flavour and moistness to these burgers, while the herbs infuse them with a freshness that's perfect for a summer meal.

Medium tomatoes, stems removed	4	4
Ketchup	3 tbsp.	45 mL
Chopped fresh chives	1 tbsp.	15 mL
Chopped fresh mint	1 tbsp.	15 mL
Crumbled feta cheese	1/2 cup	125 mL
Chopped fresh chives	2 tbsp.	30 mL
Chopped fresh mint	1 tbsp.	15 mL
Pepper	1/4 tsp.	1 mL
Salt	1/4 tsp.	1 mL
Ground turkey thigh	1 lb.	454 g
Baby arugula, lightly packed	1 cup	250 mL
Small rectangular ciabatta loaves, split and toasted, cut in half diagonally	2	2

Grill tomatoes on direct high heat for about 6 minutes, turning often, until blackened. Let stand until cool enough to handle. Remove and discard skins. Cut tomatoes in half, discarding seeds. Transfer to blender.

Add next 3 ingredients and process until combined but still slightly chunky. Makes about 1 1/4 cups (300 mL) fresh ketchup.

Combine next 6 ingredients and divide into 4 portions. Shape portions into triangular-shaped patties, about 3/4 inch (2 cm) thick to fit ciabatta wedges. Grill on direct medium-high heat for about 6 minutes per side until internal temperature reaches 175°F (80°C).

Serve patties, over a layer of arugula and topped with fresh ketchup, in ciabatta wedges. The remaining ketchup can be stored in the refrigerator for up to 1 week. Makes 4 burgers.

1 burger: 330 Calories; 12 g Total Fat (1 g Mono, 0.5 g Poly, 3.5 g Sat); 80 mg Cholesterol; 30 g Carbohydrate (2 g Fibre; 6 g Sugar); 30 g Protein; 640 mg Sodium

ABOUT KETCHUP

This favourite condiment is said to have originated in China as ke-tsiap, a spicy, fish-based mixture. The tomato-based version was introduced to North America by New Englanders in the 1700s.

Souvlaki Skewers

Succulent little skewers, marinated in fruit juices, evoke images of a rustic sea-side Mediterranean table set for friends, with the lively strains of Greek music in the background. Opa!

Large egg, fork-beaten	1	1
Fine dry bread crumbs	1/3 cup	75 mL
Finely chopped onion	1/3 cup	75 mL
Dried oregano	1 tsp.	5 mL
Grated lemon zest	1 tsp.	5 mL
Garlic clove, minced	1	1
Salt	3/4 tsp.	4 mL
Pepper	1/4 tsp.	1 mL
Ground allspice	1/4 tsp.	1 mL
Lean ground beef	1 lb.	454 g
Metal skewers (8 inches, 20 cm, each)	6	6
Apple juice	1/4 cup	60 mL
Lemon juice	3 tbsp.	45 mL
Cooking oil	2 tbsp.	30 mL
Dried oregano	2 tsp.	10 mL
Garlic clove, minced	1	1
Pepper	1/4 tsp.	1 mL

Combine first 10 ingredients and divide into 6 equal portions. Form each portion into a sausage shape, about 6 inches (15 cm) long, and insert skewers.

Combine remaining 6 ingredients in a shallow baking dish. Add skewers, cover and chill for at least 6 hours or overnight, turning occasionally. Drain and discard marinade. Grill skewers on direct medium heat for about 15 minutes, turning often, until internal temperature reaches 160°F (71°C). Makes 6 skewers.

---

1 skewer: 270 Calories; 16 g Total Fat (8 g Mono, 1.5 g Poly, 4.5 g Sat); 80 mg Cholesterol; 8 g Carbohydrate (TRACE Fibre, 2 g Sugar); 17 g Protein; 400 mg Sodium

Chicken Tikka Kabobs

Here are two ways to delight friends: invite them to a Bombay banquet, featuring these tikka kabobs, or lay out a delectable picnic with the chicken tucked into naan bread.

Plain yogurt	3/4 cup	175 mL
Finely chopped onion (see Tip, below)	2 tbsp.	30 mL
Finely grated ginger root	2 tbsp.	30 mL
Tikka curry paste	2 tbsp.	30 mL
Garlic cloves, minced	2	2
Grated lime zest	1 tsp.	5 mL
Boneless, skinless chicken breast halves, cut into 1 inch (2.5 cm) pieces	1 1/2 lbs.	680 g
Bamboo skewers (8 inches, 20 cm, each), soaked in water for 10 minutes	6	6
Chopped fresh cilantro	1 tbsp.	15 mL
Plain yogurt	1/4 cup	60 mL
Tikka curry paste	1 tbsp.	15 mL
Granulated sugar	1/2 tsp.	2 mL

Combine first 6 ingredients in a large resealable freezer bag. Add chicken and chill for at least 6 hours or overnight. Drain and discard marinade.

Thread chicken onto skewers. Grill on direct medium heat for about 18 minutes, turning occasionally, until chicken is no longer pink inside.

Combine remaining 4 ingredients. Serve with skewers. Makes 6 skewers.

---

1 skewer with 2 tsp. (10 mL) sauce: 170 Calories; 3 g Total Fat (0 g Mono, 0 g Poly, 1 g Sat); 70 mg Cholesterol; 6 g Carbohydrate (0 g Fibre, 4 g Sugar); 29 g Protein; 380 mg Sodium

TIP
To save time, use a mini food processor to finely chop the onion, ginger root and garlic.

Crab-stuffed Pepper Skewers

To delight the senses, it's all about balance. Crisp, spicy peppers pair with delicate crabmeat for a sensational combination of texture and taste. Your guests are sure to agree.

Large egg, fork-beaten	1	1
Cans of crabmeat (4 1/4 oz., 127 g, each), drained and cartilage removed, flaked	2	2
Lemon mayonnaise (see Tip, below)	3 tbsp.	45 mL
Fine dry bread crumbs	2 tbsp.	30 mL
Chopped fresh dill	1 tbsp.	15 mL
Grated lemon zest	1/2 tsp.	2 mL
Whole jalapeño peppers (about 3 inches, 7.5 cm, long), seeded (see Tip, below)	8	8
Bamboo skewers (8 inches, 20 cm, each), soaked in water for 10 minutes	8	8

Combine first 6 ingredients.

Cut a 1/2 inch (12 mm) slice lengthwise from each pepper and discard. Remove seeds and ribs. Stuff with crabmeat mixture. Thread 2 peppers onto doubled skewers, leaving a 1 inch (2.5 cm) space between them. Repeat with remaining peppers. Grill on direct medium heat for about 15 minutes until peppers are tender-crisp and internal temperature of stuffing reaches 170°F (77°C). Makes 8 stuffed peppers.

1 stuffed pepper: 80 Calories; 5 g Total Fat (2.5 g Mono, 1.5 g Poly, 0.5 g Sat); 55 mg Cholesterol; 2 g Carbohydrate (0 g Fibre, TRACE Sugar); 5 g Protein; 220 mg Sodium

TIP

To make this citrusy mayo variation yourself, simply add a little lemon juice and zest to regular mayonnaise.

TIP

The seeds and ribs of hot peppers contain capsaicin. If you like less spice in your food, removing the seeds and ribs will reduce the heat. Wear rubber gloves when handling hot peppers and avoid touching your eyes—and always wash your hands well afterwards.

Jerk Pork Rolls

This is no riddle wrapped in an enigma—just pork slices wrapped around mango and red pepper—but guests will puzzle over the easy but exquisite seasonings as you serve them eagerly anticipated seconds.

Thin mango slices (about 4 inches, 10 cm, long)	24	24
Thin red pepper slices (about 4 inches, 10 cm, long)	24	24
Chopped fresh cilantro	1/4 cup	60 mL
Boneless pork loin rib roast, frozen for 30 minutes, cut crosswise into 12 slices (see Tip, below)	1 lb.	454 g
Cooking spray		
Jerk seasoning paste	2 tbsp.	30 mL
Brown sugar, packed	2 tsp.	10 mL
Salt	1 tsp.	5 mL
Ground allspice	1/2 tsp.	2 mL

Arrange 2 mango slices and 2 red pepper slices along a short end of each pork slice. Sprinkle with cilantro. Roll up to enclose and secure with wooden picks. Spray rolls with cooking spray.

Combine remaining 4 ingredients. Rub over pork rolls. Chill, covered, for 2 hours. Grill rolls on direct medium-high heat for about 15 minutes, turning occasionally, until no longer pink inside. Makes 12 rolls.

1 roll: 90 Calories; 4 g Total Fat (2 g Mono, 0 g Poly, 1.5 g Sat); 25 mg Cholesterol; 5 g Carbohydrate (0 g Fibre, 4 g Sugar); 8 g Protein; 290 mg Sodium

TIP
Pork slices should be about 4 x 5 inches (10 x 12.5 cm) in diameter. If they are too small, place them between two sheets of plastic wrap and pound with a mallet or rolling pin until large enough.

Moroccan Fish Skewers with Lemon Beet Coulis

Warm, earthy spices give the halibut North African flair, while the sweet, tangy coulis, with its ruby-red hue, provides a pleasing contrast for the eyes and the taste buds.

Finely grated ginger root	1 tbsp.	15 mL
Ground cinnamon	1 tsp.	5 mL
Ground coriander	1 tsp.	5 mL
Ground cumin	1 tsp.	5 mL
Garlic powder	1/2 tsp.	2 mL
Salt	1/2 tsp.	2 mL
Pepper	1/2 tsp.	2 mL
Halibut fillets, skin removed and blotted dry	1 1/2 lbs.	680 g
Bamboo skewers (8 inches, 20 cm, each), soaked in water for 10 minutes	8	8
Can of whole baby beets (with liquid)	14 oz.	398 mL
Lemon juice	2 tbsp.	30 mL
Liquid honey	2 tbsp.	30 mL
Chopped fresh mint	1 tbsp.	15 mL
Grated lemon zest	1/2 tsp.	2 mL

Combine first 7 ingredients and rub over fillets. Chill, covered, for 2 hours. Cut fillets into 1 inch (2.5 cm) wide strips and thread onto skewers. Grill on direct medium-high heat for about 3 minutes per side until fish flakes easily when tested with a fork.

In a blender or food processor, process remaining 5 ingredients until smooth. Serve with skewers. Makes 8 skewers.

---

1 skewer with 1/4 cup (60 mL) coulis: 130 Calories; 2 g Total Fat (0.5 g Mono, 0.5 g Poly, 0 g Sat); 25 mg Cholesterol; 9 g Carbohydrate (1 g Fibre, 7 g Sugar); 18 g Protein; 290 mg Sodium

ABOUT COULIS
Coulis (pronounced "KOO-lee") is a thick sauce or purée. You might dress a steak with a tomato coulis, or drizzle a raspberry version over lemon cheesecake.

Apple Brandy Bratwurst Bites

A splash of apple brandy, a dollop of mustard, a lashing of cream—now here's a splendid sauce for hearty bratwursts. Snuggle these fellows onto a bed of sautéed onions and watch your guests' eyes light up!

Apple juice	1/2 cup	125 mL
Apple brandy (such as Calvados)	1/3 cup	75 mL
Brown sugar, packed	2 tbsp.	30 mL
Dijon mustard	2 tsp.	10 mL
Salt	1/4 tsp.	1 mL
Half-and-half cream	1/4 cup	60 mL
Thinly sliced red onion	2 cups	500 mL
Precooked bratwurst sausages, cut into 8 pieces each	4	4
Poultry lacers (see Tip, page 10)	8	8

Combine first 5 ingredients in a saucepan. Gently boil on medium until reduced by half. Stir in cream. Keep warm.

Cook onion in greased preheated barbecue wok on direct medium-high heat for 25 to 30 minutes, stirring occasionally, until soft and browned.

Thread sausage pieces onto lacers. Grill on direct medium-high heat for about 12 minutes, turning often, until heated through and browned. Arrange skewers over onions on a serving plate. Drizzle with half of apple cream sauce, serving remainder on the side. Makes 8 skewers.

1 skewer with 1 tbsp. (15 mL) sauce: 210 Calories; 13 g Total Fat (0 g Mono, 0 g Poly, 5 g Sat); 35 mg Cholesterol; 9 g Carbohydrate (0 g Fibre, 6 g Sugar); 8 g Protein; 500 mg Sodium

ABOUT BRATWURST

This German sausage is traditionally made with veal, pork and a blend of sweet and savoury spices.

Cajun Chicken Wings

Your friends will love the spicy, sweet coating on these tasty wings. Transport them to New Orleans and enjoy the easy days—and flavours—of summer.

Whole chicken wings, tips attached	12	12
Bamboo skewers (8 inches, 20 cm, each), soaked in water for 10 minutes	12	12
Brown sugar, packed	2 tbsp.	30 mL
Smoked sweet paprika	4 tsp.	20 mL
Dried oregano	2 tsp.	10 mL
Dried thyme	2 tsp.	10 mL
Garlic salt	2 tsp.	10 mL
Onion powder	2 tsp.	10 mL
Ground allspice	1 tsp.	5 mL
Ground ginger	1 tsp.	5 mL
Cayenne pepper	1/2 tsp.	2 mL
Mayonnaise	2/3 cup	150 mL
Lime juice	2 tbsp.	30 mL
Brown sugar, packed	1 tbsp.	15 mL
Chopped fresh chives	1 tbsp.	15 mL

Straighten each wing. Thread skewer lengthwise through base of drumette to tip of wing.

Combine next 9 ingredients and sprinkle over wings. Chill, covered, for 2 hours. Grill on direct medium heat for about 25 minutes, turning occasionally, until crisp and no longer pink at the bone.

Stir remaining 4 ingredients until smooth. Serve with wings. Makes 12 wings.

---

1 wing with 1 tbsp. (15 mL) mayonnaise mixture: 220 Calories; 17 g Total Fat (8 g Mono, 4.5 g Poly, 3 g Sat); 40 mg Cholesterol; 5 g Carbohydrate (0 g Fibre, 4 g Sugar); 9 g Protein; 410 mg Sodium

Sesame Scallops with Maple Cream

East meets West with these delectable scallops, served with a sauce of North American maple syrup and Japanese ponzu sauce. International relations have never tasted so good!

Sesame oil	2 tbsp.	30 mL
Soy sauce	4 tsp.	20 mL
Pepper	1/2 tsp.	2 mL
Jumbo scallops (about 1 1/2 oz., 43 g, each)	12	12
Lemon mayonnaise	6 tbsp.	100 mL
Maple syrup	2 tsp.	10 mL
Ponzu sauce	2 tsp.	10 mL
Wooden skewers (4 inches, 10 cm, each), soaked in water for 10 minutes	6	6

Combine first 3 ingredients in a large resealable freezer bag. Add scallops and chill for 30 minutes. Drain and discard marinade.

Stir next 3 ingredients together until smooth.

Thread 2 scallops onto each skewer. Grill on direct high heat for 3 to 4 minutes per side until scallops are just opaque. Serve with mayonnaise mixture. Makes 6 skewers.

1 skewer with 1 tbsp. (15 mL) mayonnaise mixture: 220 Calories; 15 g Total Fat (8 g Mono, 5 g Poly, 1.5 g Sat); 35 mg Cholesterol; 3 g Carbohydrate (0 g Fibre, 1 g Sugar); 15 g Protein; 480 mg Sodium

MAKE AHEAD
Mayonnaise mixture can be made ahead of time and stored in the refrigerator.

Saltimbocca Skewers with Arugula Salad

This charming Italian word, saltimbocca, literally means "jumps in the mouth." Savour the experience with this combination of fresh sage, prosciutto, veal and a touch of honey.

Veal scaloppine	1 lb.	454 g
Pepper	1/8 tsp.	0.5 mL
Prosciutto ham slices, halved lengthwise	6	6
Fresh sage leaves	36	36
Metal skewers (8 – 10 inches, 20 – 25 cm, each)	12	12
Olive oil	1 tbsp.	15 mL
Lemon juice	1 tbsp.	15 mL
Liquid honey	1 tsp.	5 mL
Salt	1/8 tsp.	0.5 mL
Pepper, just a pinch		
Arugula leaves, lightly packed	4 cups	1 L

Cut scaloppine into 12 pieces, about 2 inches (5 cm) wide and 8 inches (20 cm) long. Sprinkle with pepper.

Arrange 1 prosciutto slice over each piece of veal, topping each with 3 sage leaves. Pound lightly to adhere layers. Thread onto skewers, accordion-style, making sure the sage leaves are secured. Grill, starting veal-side down, on direct medium-high heat for about 3 minutes per side until veal is no longer pink.

Combine next 5 ingredients. Add arugula and toss. Arrange on a serving plate and top with skewers. Makes 12 skewers.

---

1 skewer with 1/3 cup (75 mL) salad: 100 Calories; 6 g Total Fat (2 g Mono, 0 g Poly, 2 g Sat); 40 mg Cholesterol; TRACE Carbohydrate (0 g Fibre, TRACE Sugar); 10 g Protein; 270 mg Sodium

Rosemary-skewered Seafood

Lovely pink and white morsels from the sea skewered onto sprigs of aromatic rosemary and brushed with a tart glaze—these kabobs will be the highlight of any evening.

Fresh rosemary sprigs (about 4 inches, 10 cm), soaked in water for 10 minutes	8	8
Large sea scallops	8	8
Uncooked large shrimp (peeled and deveined)	8	8
Pink grapefruit juice	3 tbsp.	45 mL
Extra-virgin olive oil	2 tbsp.	30 mL
Liquid honey	2 tsp.	10 mL
Grated grapefruit zest	1/2 tsp.	2 mL
Finely chopped fresh rosemary	1/4 tsp.	1 mL
Salt, sprinkle		
Pepper, sprinkle		

Remove lower leaves of rosemary sprigs (see Tip, below) and thread 1 scallop and 1 shrimp onto each sprig.

Combine remaining 7 ingredients and brush over scallops and shrimp. Grill on direct medium-high heat for about 2 minutes per side, brushing with any remaining grapefruit juice mixture, until shrimp turn pink and scallops are opaque. Makes 8 skewers.

---

1 skewer: 90 Calories; 4 g Total Fat (3 g Mono, 0 g Poly, 0.5 g Sat); 25 mg Cholesterol; 3 g Carbohydrate (0 g Fibre, 1 g Sugar); 10 g Protein; 135 mg Sodium

TIP
Use some of the rosemary leaves you remove from the skewers to chop and add to the grapefruit juice mixture.

Bourbon Pepper-crusted Salmon

Entertaining has never been easier—toss some lightly oiled bell pepper pieces onto the grill next to the cedar-planked salmon, then join your guests for pre-dinner drinks.

Salmon fillet, skin-on	1 1/2 lbs.	680 g
Cedar plank, soaked in water for 4 hours	1	1
Fine dry bread crumbs	3 tbsp.	45 mL
Brown sugar, packed	2 tbsp.	30 mL
Bourbon	1 tbsp.	15 mL
Thick teriyaki sauce	2 tsp.	10 mL
Coarsely ground pepper	1 tsp.	5 mL

Place salmon, skin-side down, on cedar plank (see Tip, below).

Combine next 5 ingredients and spread over salmon. Prepare grill for direct medium-high heat. Place salmon and plank on grill. Reduce heat to medium-low and cook salmon for about 14 minutes until fish flakes easily when tested with a fork. Serves 6.

---

1 serving: 200 Calories; 7 g Total Fat (2.5 g Mono, 3 g Poly, 1 g Sat); 60 mg Cholesterol; 8 g Carbohydrate (0 g Fibre, 5 g Sugar); 23 g Protein; 110 mg Sodium

TIP
Have a spray bottle of water handy to douse any flames if the plank happens to catch fire.

ABOUT PLANKS
Salmon is often cooked on cedar, but other kinds of wood, such as alder, hickory, maple and oak may also be used. Using the oak staves of old wine barrels can infuse the fish with wine flavour as it cooks. Make sure whatever plank you use is clean, unvarnished and comes from non-resinous wood.

Smoked Fennel Trout

Any recipe worth its salt offers intriguing tastes and a satisfying outcome. This brined trout, flavoured with fennel seed and lemon, will reward your culinary curiosity on both counts.

Water	4 cups	1 L
Chopped onion	1 cup	250 mL
Coarse salt	2/3 cup	150 mL
Fennel seed, crushed	2 tbsp.	30 mL
Garlic cloves, minced	2	2
Whole rainbow trout (7 – 8 oz., 200 – 225 g, each), pan-ready	4	4
Fennel seed, crushed	2 tsp.	10 mL
Lemon slices, halved	8	8
Apple wood chips, soaked in water for 1 hour and drained	2 cups	500 mL
Fennel seed, soaked in water for 1 hour and drained	1 tbsp.	15 mL

Stir first 5 ingredients in 9 × 13 inch (23 × 33 cm) baking dish until salt is dissolved. Add fish and cover with plastic wrap. Set a cutting board over top and use a weight to keep fish submerged in brine. Chill for 1 hour. Drain and discard brine. Rinse fish and pat dry.

Sprinkle second amount of fennel seed in cavity of fish and fill with lemon slices.

Put wood chips and third amount of fennel seed into smoker box. Prepare grill for indirect medium heat with smoker box. Cook fish for about 10 minutes per side until it flakes easily when tested with a fork. Serves 8.

---

1 serving: 140 Calories; 4 g Total Fat (1.5 g Mono, 1.5 g Poly, 1 g Sat); 65 mg Cholesterol; 2 g Carbohydrate (TRACE Fibre, 0 g Sugar); 23 g Protein; 880 mg Sodium

ABOUT BRINING
Immersing fish in a higher-concentration salt solution allows the fish to absorb the liquid and to be infused by the flavours it contains. When cooked, brined fish retains much of this moisture.

EXPERIMENT!
This dish is also delicious served cold.

Grilled Red Snapper with Lime Butter

The sharp tang and buttery richness of the lime butter bring a fascinating note to this vividly seasoned snapper, creating culinary harmony on the dinner plate.

Butter, softened	1/4 cup	60 mL
Grated lime zest	1 tsp.	5 mL
Lime juice	1 tsp.	5 mL
Coarsely ground pepper	1/2 tsp.	2 mL
Lime juice	2 tbsp.	30 mL
Tex-Mex seasoning	2 tbsp.	30 mL
Brown sugar, packed	1 tbsp.	15 mL
Olive oil	1 tbsp.	15 mL
Coarse salt	1 tsp.	5 mL
Red snapper fillets	1 1/2 lbs.	680 g

Beat first 4 ingredients until creamy. Spoon onto a sheet of waxed paper and form into a 2 inch (5 cm) long cylinder (see How To, below). Wrap tightly and freeze for about 1 hour until firm.

Combine next 5 ingredients and spread over fillets. Chill, covered, for 30 minutes. Place fillets on a sheet of greased heavy-duty (or double layer of regular) foil. Cook on direct medium heat for 8 to 10 minutes until fish flakes easily when tested with a fork. Serve with sliced lime butter medallions. Serves 6.

---

1 serving: 220 Calories; 11 g Total Fat (4 g Mono, 1 g Poly, 5 g Sat); 60 mg Cholesterol; 5 g Carbohydrate (0 g Fibre, 2 g Sugar); 23 g Protein; 650 mg Sodium

HOW TO MAKE A BUTTER LOG

To roll butter into a log easily, place butter mixture onto centre of a sheet of waxed (or parchment) paper. Fold half of paper over butter mixture. Using a straight edge, such as a ruler, press paper under butter mixture to make a cylinder. Twist ends of paper. Wrap in plastic wrap if storing for a longer period of time in the freezer.

Herbed Bulgur-stuffed Calamari

Indulge your spirit of adventure—and your taste buds—with tender squid stuffed with fresh herbs and lemon-scented bulgur. What a stunning addition to any Mediterranean meal.

Olive oil	1 tsp.	5 mL
Finely chopped red pepper	1 cup	250 mL
Finely diced onion	1 cup	250 mL
Coarsely chopped pine nuts	1/4 cup	60 mL
Garlic cloves, minced	2	2
Salt	1/2 tsp.	2 mL
Cooked bulgur (see Tip, below)	1 1/2 cups	375 mL
Finely chopped fresh oregano	2 tbsp.	30 mL
Finely chopped parsley	1 tbsp.	15 mL
Grated lemon zest	1 tsp.	5 mL
Squid tubes (about 4 inches, 10 cm, long)	12	12
Wooden picks	12	12
Olive oil	1 tbsp.	15 mL
Salt, sprinkle		
Pepper, sprinkle		

Heat olive oil in a saucepan on medium. Add next 5 ingredients and cook for about 5 minutes until red pepper is tender-crisp.

Add bulgur and stir until heated through. Remove from heat and stir in next 3 ingredients. Transfer to a medium freezer bag with a small piece snipped off 1 corner.

Turn squid tubes inside out (see How To, below) and score lightly in cross-hatch pattern with the tip of a sharp knife (see Why To, below). Fill squid tubes with bulgur mixture. Secure larger open ends with wooden picks. Brush with olive oil and sprinkle with salt and pepper. Grill on direct medium-high heat for about 5 minutes, turning often, until squid just turns opaque. Do not overcook. Makes 12 stuffed calamari.

---

1 stuffed calamari: 90 Calories; 4 g Total Fat (1.5 g Mono, 1 g Poly, 0 g Sat); 45 mg Cholesterol; 11 g Carbohydrate (3 g Fibre, 1 g Sugar); 5 g Protein; 110 mg Sodium

HOW TO TURN SQUID
Use the handle of a wooden spoon to turn the end of the squid to the inside.

WHY TO
Cross-hatching the inside—the fleshier part—of the squid helps to tenderize it.

TIP
For every one part fine bulgur, use 1 1/2 parts water. Bring water to a boil in saucepan. Add bulgur and remove from heat. Let stand, covered, for 30 minutes.

Maple Walnut Arctic Char

Humans boast five taste receptors: sweet, salty, sour, bitter and umami, or savoury. This dish, featuring maple syrup, seasoned salt, apple cider vinegar, arugula leaves and arctic char, is sure to enliven them all.

Butter	1 tsp.	5 mL
Maple syrup	1 tbsp.	15 mL
Walnut halves, toasted (see How To, page 132)	1/2 cup	125 mL
Finely chopped walnuts	1/2 cup	125 mL
Maple syrup	1/4 cup	60 mL
Dijon mustard (with whole seeds)	1 tbsp.	15 mL
Seasoned salt	1 tsp.	5 mL
Garlic powder	1/2 tsp.	2 mL
Pepper	1/2 tsp.	2 mL
Arctic char fillets (5 – 6 oz., 140 – 170 g, each), blotted dry	4	4
Arugula leaves, lightly packed	3 cups	750 mL
Apple cider vinegar	3 tbsp.	45 mL
Maple syrup	3 tbsp.	45 mL

Heat butter and maple syrup in a saucepan on medium until butter is melted. Add walnut halves and stir until coated. Spread on a plate to cool.

Combine next 6 ingredients and spread over fillets. Cook on indirect high heat (see Why To, below) for about 10 minutes until fish flakes easily when tested with a fork.

Arrange arugula on a large serving platter. Combine vinegar and syrup and drizzle over arugula. Sprinkle with candied walnuts and arrange fillets in centre of plate. Serves 4.

1 serving: 540 Calories; 33 g Total Fat (3 g Mono, 14 g Poly, 2.5 g Sat); 35 mg Cholesterol; 26 g Carbohydrate (2 g Fibre, 20 g Sugar); 40 g Protein; 550 mg Sodium

WHY TO
Cooking the fish on indirect high heat prevents the sugary crust from burning and allows the nuts to become crisp.

ABOUT ARCTIC CHAR
Related to trout and salmon, arctic char lives in cold ocean waters and sometimes in deep, circumpolar, freshwater lakes. However, most char sold to North Americans is raised in farms in the North Atlantic. Its delicate pink (sometimes white) flesh tastes like a cross between trout and salmon and may be cooked in a variety of ways. If arctic char is unavailable, try this recipe using salmon.

Woven Salmon and Halibut with Tahini Tartar Sauce

Mothers may be right most times, but here's a stunning reason to go ahead and play with your food. Creating this lovely lattice takes only minutes, but its appeal will be long lasting.

Plain yogurt	2/3 cup	150 mL
Tahini	1/3 cup	75 mL
Capers	2 tbsp.	30 mL
Finely chopped gherkins	2 tbsp.	30 mL
Finely chopped roasted red pepper	2 tbsp.	30 mL
Lemon juice	2 tbsp.	30 mL
Mayonnaise	2 tbsp.	30 mL
Garlic clove, minced	1	1
Halibut fillets (1/2 – 3/4 inch, 1.2 – 2 cm, thick), cut into 1/2 inch (12 mm) wide strips	3/4 lb.	340 g
Salmon fillets (1/2 – 3/4 inch, 1.2 – 2 cm, thick), cut into 1/2 inch (12 mm) wide strips	3/4 lb.	340 g
Melted butter	3 tbsp.	45 mL
Lemon juice	2 tbsp.	30 mL
Chopped fresh dill	2 tsp.	10 mL
Coarsely ground pepper	1/2 tsp.	2 mL

Combine first 8 ingredients and chill for 30 minutes to blend flavours.

Place halibut on greased broiler rack, leaving spaces between strips. Weave salmon over and under halibut.

Combine remaining 4 ingredients and brush over fish. Place fish on rack over grill. Cook on direct medium-high heat for about 10 minutes, brushing occasionally with any remaining butter mixture, until fish flakes easily when tested with a fork. Serve with yogurt mixture. Serves 6.

1 serving: 360 Calories; 22 g Total Fat (5 g Mono, 3 g Poly, 6 g Sat); 70 mg Cholesterol; 11 g Carbohydrate (2 g Fibre, 5 g Sugar); 27 g Protein; 340 mg Sodium

ABOUT BUYING FISH FILLETS
To ensure you're buying fresh fish, check that:
- the flesh colour is bright and consistent
- the fish smells fresh and not "fishy"
- the flesh is firm, elastic and moist—but not slimy
- the cut edges are neat and clean

Jerk Bass Fillets

Two citrus fruits for twice the zest—tucked into a package with allspice, brown sugar, jerk seasoning and sea bass. Served with grilled slices of lime and orange, this fish truly animates the senses.

Jerk seasoning paste	2 tbsp.	30 mL
Brown sugar, packed	1 tbsp.	15 mL
Ground allspice	1/2 tsp.	2 mL
Grated lime zest	1/2 tsp.	2 mL
Grated orange zest	1/2 tsp.	2 mL
Sea bass fillets (5 – 6 oz., 140 – 170 g, each), blotted dry	4	4
Lime slices (about 1/4 inch, 6 mm, thick), blotted dry	6	6
Orange slices (about 1/4 inch, 6 mm, thick), blotted dry	6	6

Combine first 5 ingredients and rub over fillets. Chill, covered, for 2 hours. Place fillets in greased foil pan and cover tightly with foil. Cook on direct medium-high heat for about 15 minutes until fish flakes easily when tested with a fork.

Grill lime and orange slices on direct medium-high heat for 2 to 3 minutes per side until browned. Arrange fillets with lime and orange slices on a large serving plate. Serves 4.

1 serving: 180 Calories; 4 g Total Fat (0.5 g Mono, 1 g Poly, 1 g Sat); 60 mg Cholesterol; 9 g Carbohydrate (1 g Fibre, 5 g Sugar); 26 g Protein; 200 mg Sodium

ABOUT JERK COOKING
Jerk meat dishes are most closely associated with Jamaican cuisine. According to tradition, chicken, pork and fish are rubbed and marinated with a spicy seasoning and cooked over a coal fire overlaid with the wood or berries of the pimento (or allspice) tree.

Seared Tuna Steak with Sesame Ginger Sauce

Sesame, ginger and sake provide a Japanese essence to fresh tuna steak. The charred smokiness of the baby bok choy takes this to another level.

Ponzu sauce	2 tbsp.	30 mL
Tahini	2 tbsp.	30 mL
Finely grated ginger root	1 tbsp.	15 mL
Sake	1 tbsp.	15 mL
Sesame oil	1 tbsp.	15 mL
Garlic clove, minced	1	1
Dry mustard	1/2 tsp.	2 mL
Ponzu sauce	1/4 cup	60 mL
Sake	2 tbsp.	30 mL
Sesame oil	2 tbsp.	30 mL
Finely chopped fresh chives	1 tbsp.	15 mL
Tuna steaks (4 – 6 oz., 113 – 170 g, each), about 1 inch (2.5 cm) thick	4	4
Whole baby bok choy, halved lengthwise	8	8

Combine first 7 ingredients. Set aside.

Combine next 4 ingredients. Reserve 1/4 cup (60 mL). Pour remaining mixture into a large resealable freezer bag. Add tuna and chill for 30 minutes. Drain and discard marinade.

Grill tuna and bok choy on direct medium-high heat for about 3 minutes per side, brushing with reserved marinade, until tuna is medium-rare and bok choy is tender-crisp. Serve with ponzu tahini mixture. Serves 4.

---

1 serving: 390 Calories; 21 g Total Fat (6 g Mono, 6 g Poly, 3.5 g Sat); 55 mg Cholesterol; 9 g Carbohydrate (2 g Fibre, 4 g Sugar); 37 g Protein; 720 mg Sodium

ABOUT PONZU SAUCE

A common ingredient in Japanese cooking, ponzu is made from a mixture of soy sauce, lemon juice or rice vinegar, kombu (seaweed), dried bonito flakes and mirin or sake. It is generally used as a dipping sauce.

MAKE AHEAD

Prepare the sauce in advance and store in the refrigerator. Bring to room temperature before serving.

Mussels in Spicy Coconut Broth

A bowl full of richly spiced mussels can stretch out an evening, as friends hunt for plump treasures inside luminescent shells. Linger, laugh and enjoy the company.

Mussels	2 lbs.	900 g
Can of coconut milk	14 oz.	398 mL
Lime juice	2 tbsp.	30 mL
Soy sauce	1 tbsp.	15 mL
Thai hot chili peppers, finely chopped (see Tip, page 64)	3	3

Lightly tap to close any mussels that are opened 1/4 inch (6 mm) or more (see About Mussels, below). Discard any that do not close. Put mussels into 9 × 13 inch (23 × 33 cm) foil pan.

Combine remaining 4 ingredients in a saucepan and bring to a boil. Pour over mussels and cover pan tightly with foil. Cook on direct high heat for 6 to 8 minutes until mussels are opened. Discard any unopened mussels. Transfer mussels with cooking liquid to a serving bowl. Serves 6.

1 serving: 270 Calories; 17 g Total Fat (1.5 g Mono, 1 g Poly, 13 g Sat); 40 mg Cholesterol; 10 g Carbohydrate (0 g Fibre, 1 g Sugar); 20 g Protein; 600 mg Sodium

ABOUT MUSSELS

For great flavour and to maintain food safety, there are a few important points to keep in mind when cooking with mussels:

- Only use mussels with tightly closed shells. If the shells are slightly open, tap them lightly. If they don't close, don't use them.
- Discard any mussels with broken shells.
- Avoid mussels that feel heavy; they may be filled with sand. Also avoid mussels that feel too light, or that are loose when shaken.
- Shucked mussels should be plump, with clear liquid.
- Smaller mussels tend to be more tender than larger ones.
- Discard any mussels that do not open during cooking.

Lemon Ginger Halibut

Sip some sake with your dinner guests while the halibut cooks to moist, flaky perfection. Savour the aroma of lemon and ginger rising in the air. You're just moments away from experiencing the Asian-inspired flavours mingling on the grill.

Sake	1/4 cup	60 mL
Lemon juice	3 tbsp.	45 mL
Brown sugar, packed	2 tbsp.	30 mL
Cooking oil	1 tbsp.	15 mL
Finely grated ginger root	1 tbsp.	15 mL
Soy sauce	1 tbsp.	15 mL
Garlic cloves, minced	2	2
Grated lemon zest (see Tip, below)	2 tsp.	10 mL
Chili paste (sambal oelek)	1/2 tsp.	2 mL
Halibut fillets (about 1 inch, 2.5 cm, thick), about 4 – 5 oz. (113 – 140 g), each	6	6
Finely chopped green onion	1 tbsp.	15 mL

Combine first 9 ingredients in a large resealable freezer bag.

Add fillets and chill for 30 minutes. Drain marinade into a saucepan. Simmer on medium-low until slightly thickened. Grill fillets on direct medium heat for about 4 minutes per side, brushing with thickened marinade, until fish flakes easily when tested with a fork.

Sprinkle with green onion. Serves 6.

1 serving: 200 Calories; 5 g Total Fat (2.5 g Mono, 1.5 g Poly, 0.5 g Sat); 40 mg Cholesterol; 6 g Carbohydrate (0 g Fibre, 5 g Sugar); 27 g Protein; 230 mg Sodium

TIP

When a recipe calls for grated citrus zest and juice, it's easier to grate the zest first, then juice. Be careful not to grate down to the pith (the white part of the peel), which is bitter and best avoided.

Cherry-glazed Salmon

Enjoy the burst of sweet and tart from the cherries and balsamic vinegar. Lightly dressed summer greens, crusty bread and a cold glass of white Zinfandel round out the menu for a patio meal.

Cherry jam	1/2 cup	125 mL
Pitted sour cherries, drained	1/2 cup	125 mL
Balsamic vinegar	2 tbsp.	30 mL
Coarsely ground pepper	2 tsp.	10 mL
Salt	1/2 tsp.	2 mL
Salmon fillet, skin-on	1 1/2 lbs.	680 g

In a blender or food processor, process first 5 ingredients until almost smooth. Transfer to a saucepan and gently boil on medium until reduced and very thick. Set aside.

Place fillet, skin-side down, on a sheet of greased heavy-duty (or double layer of regular) foil (see Tip, below). Cook on direct medium-high heat for 10 minutes. Spoon cherry mixture over top. Cook for about 10 minutes more until fish flakes easily when tested with a fork. Serves 6.

1 serving: 250 Calories; 7 g Total Fat (2.5 g Mono, 3 g Poly, 1 g Sat); 60 mg Cholesterol; 23 g Carbohydrate (0 g Fibre, 21 g Sugar); 23 g Protein; 250 mg Sodium

TIP
Cooking the salmon on foil makes transferring it to the serving plate quick and easy.

Chai-smoked Chicken

Conjure up the markets of New Delhi as the scent of chai mingles with the enticing aroma of chicken sizzling on the grill. The wood chips provide a rich, smoky bouquet with a subtle maple undertone.

Unsweetened chai tea concentrate	1 cup	250 mL
Whole chicken, halved, backbone and breastbone removed (see How To, below)	3 lbs.	1.4 kg
Maple wood chips, soaked in water for 1 hour and drained	2 cups	500 mL
Brown sugar, packed	1/2 cup	125 mL
Chai tea leaves	5 tsp.	25 mL

Pour tea concentrate into a large resealable freezer bag. Add chicken and chill for at least 6 hours or overnight.

Combine next 3 ingredients in smoker box. Prepare grill for indirect medium heat with a drip pan and smoker box. Drain and discard marinade. Cook chicken, skin-side down, for about 20 minutes. Turn and cook for about 20 minutes more until internal temperature reaches 170°F (77°C). Cover with foil and let stand for 10 minutes. Serves 4.

1 serving: 250 Calories; 10 g Total Fat (3.5 g Mono, 2 g Poly, 2.5 g Sat); 115 mg Cholesterol; 0 g Carbohydrate (0 g Fibre, 0 g Sugar); 38 g Protein; 112 mg Sodium

HOW TO REMOVE BACKBONE AND HALVE CHICKEN
Cut along both sides of backbone to remove.

Pomegranate Chili Chicken

When a fruit evokes images of rubies and garnets, you know the meal it garnishes is worthy of royalty—or good friends. Pomegranate seeds add the final touch to this entree dressed up with a sweet, tangy sauce.

Pomegranate juice	2 cups	500 mL
Granulated sugar	1/4 cup	60 mL
Dried crushed chilies	1 tsp.	5 mL
Boneless, skinless chicken breast halves (4 – 6 oz., 113 – 170 g, each)	4	4
Cooking spray		
Garlic powder	1 tsp.	5 mL
Ground cumin	1 tsp.	5 mL
Ground ginger	1 tsp.	5 mL
Seasoned salt	1 tsp.	5 mL
Arugula leaves, lightly packed	1 cup	250 mL

Combine first 3 ingredients in a saucepan. Gently boil on medium until reduced to about 1/2 cup (125 mL). Reserve 1/4 cup (60 mL).

Spray chicken with cooking spray. Combine next 4 ingredients and rub over chicken. Grill on direct medium heat for about 6 minutes per side, brushing occasionally with remaining pomegranate mixture, until internal temperature reaches 170°F (77°C).

Arrange arugula on a serving plate and top with chicken. Drizzle with reserved pomegranate mixture. Serves 4.

---

1 serving: 290 Calories; 2 g Total Fat (0 g Mono, 0 g Poly, 0 g Sat); 80 mg Cholesterol; 33 g Carbohydrate (0 g Fibre, 31 g Sugar); 33 g Protein; 640 mg Sodium

ABOUT POMEGRANATES
This fruit symbolizes abundance and fertility in some Mediterranean cultures. Pomegranates are in season from fall to winter and can usually be found in abundance in grocery stores in November and December.

MAKE AHEAD
The glaze can be made one or two days in advance. Bring it to room temperature before using.

Buttery Spiced Chicken

The charms of India are evident in the choice of aromatic spices, delivered in a buttery basting sauce. Add some incense to a corner of the patio and a bowl of marigold petals to the table for extra atmosphere.

Melted butter	1/4 cup	60 mL
Ground coriander	1 tbsp.	15 mL
Ground ginger	1 tbsp.	15 mL
Dried crushed chilies	1 1/2 tsp.	7 mL
Ground cumin	1 1/2 tsp.	7 mL
Garlic powder	3/4 tsp.	4 mL
Salt	3/4 tsp.	4 mL
Chicken legs, thighs attached (11 – 12 oz., 310 – 340 g, each), skin removed (see Tip, below)	4	4

Combine first 7 ingredients.

Prepare grill for indirect medium heat. Cook chicken over lit burner for about 10 minutes per side until browned. Brush with butter mixture, then place chicken, bone-side down, over unlit burner. Cook for another 30 to 35 minutes until internal temperature reaches 170°F (77°C). Makes 4 legs.

---

1 leg: 510 Calories; 28 g Total Fat (8 g Mono, 4.5 g Poly, 11 g Sat); 280 mg Cholesterol; 2 g Carbohydrate (TRACE Fibre, 0 g Sugar); 60 g Protein; 800 mg Sodium

TIP
When removing chicken skin, use a paper towel to grip the chicken leg.

Twist of Lime Chicken with Three-tomato Salsa

Fresh, grilled and sun-dried tomatoes—what a feast for fans of what the Italians call "apples of gold." This salsa is splendid with these chicken breasts, but you'll soon be spooning it over your favourite burgers and smokies too.

Medium tomatoes, cut into 1/2 inch (12 mm) slices	2	2
Medium onion, cut into 1/2 inch (12 mm) slices	1	1
Olive oil	1 tbsp.	15 mL
Salt, sprinkle		
Pepper, sprinkle		
Chopped tomato	1/2 cup	125 mL
Sun-dried tomatoes in oil, blotted dry, chopped	1/4 cup	60 mL
Chopped fresh cilantro	2 tbsp.	30 mL
Lime juice	1 tbsp.	15 mL
Red wine vinegar	1 tbsp.	15 mL
Granulated sugar	1 tsp.	5 mL
Lime juice	2 tbsp.	30 mL
Olive oil	1 tbsp.	15 mL
Ground cumin	1 tsp.	5 mL
Hot pepper sauce	1/2 tsp.	2 mL
Salt	1/2 tsp.	2 mL
Pepper	1/2 tsp.	2 mL
Boneless, skinless chicken breast halves (4 – 6 oz., 113 – 170 g, each)	4	4

Brush first amount of tomato and onion with olive oil. Sprinkle with salt and pepper. Grill on direct medium-high heat for 5 to 10 minutes per side until softened and grill marks appear. Let stand until cool enough to handle. Chop onion and tomato.

Add next 6 ingredients and stir well. Chill.

Combine next 6 ingredients in a large resealable freezer bag. Add chicken and chill for 1 hour. Drain and discard marinade. Grill chicken on direct medium-high heat for about 8 minutes per side until internal temperature reaches 170°F (77°C). Cover with foil and let stand for 5 minutes. Serve with tomato mixture. Serves 4.

1 serving: 270 Calories; 10 g Total Fat (6 g Mono, 1.5 g Poly, 1.5 g Sat); 80 mg Cholesterol; 10 g Carbohydrate (2 g Fibre, 5 g Sugar); 34 g Protein; 410 mg Sodium

Wine "Poached" Chicken with Rosemary Garlic Vegetables

Here's an uptown version of beer can chicken that calls for an infusion of "Scarborough Fair" herbs: parsley, sage, rosemary and thyme. Guests will remember this meal with pleasure.

Baby carrots	1 lb.	454 g
Multi-coloured baby potatoes	1 lb.	454 g
Chopped fresh rosemary	1 tbsp.	15 mL
Olive oil	1 tbsp.	15 mL
Garlic cloves, minced	2	2
Salt	1/4 tsp.	1 mL
Pepper	1/4 tsp.	1 mL
Dry white wine	1 1/4 cups	300 mL
Sprigs of fresh parsley	2	2
Sprigs of fresh thyme	2	2
Sprig of fresh rosemary	1	1
Sprig of fresh sage	1	1
Olive oil	1 tbsp.	15 mL
Whole roasting chicken	4 lbs.	1.8 kg
Seasoned salt	1 tsp.	5 mL

Combine first 7 ingredients. Microwave, covered, on high (100%) for about 15 minutes until tender.

Punch 3 holes in top of clean, empty beer or soda can and fill with next 5 ingredients. Place can in roasting stand (see Tip, below).

Rub olive oil over surface of chicken. Sprinkle skin and cavity with seasoned salt. Stand the chicken, tail-end down, over can and press down to insert can into body cavity. Prepare grill for indirect medium heat with a drip pan. Place a barbecue wok over the drip pan. Place chicken on roasting stand in the centre of the wok. Cook for 45 minutes. Add vegetables to wok and cook for another 45 minutes, stirring occasionally, until vegetables are tender and meat thermometer inserted into chicken thigh reads 180°F (82°C). Carefully remove wok and chicken. Cover with foil and let stand for 10 minutes. Remove vegetables to a serving platter. Carefully remove chicken from roasting stand. Place over vegetables. The liquid in the can will be very hot. Serves 6.

1 serving: 810 Calories; 50 g Total Fat (22 g Mono, 10 g Poly, 14 g Sat); 225 mg Cholesterol; 21 g Carbohydrate (2 g Fibre, 4 g Sugar); 58 g Protein; 630 mg Sodium

TIP
Take advantage of special grilling accessories such as the beer can chicken stand, which balances the chicken upright on the barbecue. Woks, grilling baskets and roasters designed for use on the barbecue are also available. If you can't find these items in your department store, there are several online barbecue specialty shops that supply them.

Cinnamon Cherry Duck Breasts

The rich, complex flavours of duck are underscored here with a sweet cherry sauce. The grilling technique ensures moist, tasty meat and crispy skin.

Cherry jam	1/2 cup	125 mL
Dry red wine	1/4 cup	60 mL
Red wine vinegar	1 tbsp.	15 mL
Ground cinnamon	1/4 tsp.	1 mL
Salt	1/8 tsp.	0.5 mL
Pitted sour cherries	1/2 cup	125 mL
Bone-in duck breast halves (14 – 16 oz., 395 – 454 g, each)	4	4
Ground cinnamon	1 tbsp.	15 mL
Brown sugar, packed	1 tsp.	5 mL
Seasoned salt	1 tsp.	5 mL
Cherry wood chips, soaked in water for 1 hour and drained	2 cups	500 mL

Combine first 5 ingredients in a saucepan. Simmer on medium-low for 10 minutes to blend flavours. Stir in cherries.

Score duck skin in a cross-hatch pattern, taking care not to cut into the meat. Combine next 3 ingredients and rub over the skin and meat.

Put wood chips into smoker box. Prepare grill for indirect medium heat with a drip pan and smoker box. Cook duck, skin-side up, for 60 to 70 minutes until internal temperature reaches 170°F (77°C). Cover with foil and let stand for 10 minutes. Serve with cherry mixture. Serves 4.

1 serving: 640 Calories; 17 g Total Fat (4.5 g Mono, 2.5 g Poly, 5 g Sat); 305 mg Cholesterol; 36 g Carbohydrate (1 g Fibre, 32 g Sugar); 79 g Protein; 680 mg Sodium

ABOUT DUCK

Don't confuse duck meat with chicken—duck is much fattier, darker and more flavourful. For safety reasons, duck should be cooked to medium-well, or 170°F (77°C).

Coconut Pesto-stuffed Chicken Breasts

Whisk friends to the tropics with chicken breasts stuffed with a coconut pesto. The coconut-rum wash gives the chicken a deep caramelized colour and just a touch of "spirited" flavour.

Fresh basil, lightly packed	1 1/2 cups	375 mL
Chopped macadamia nuts	1/3 cup	75 mL
Medium sweetened coconut	1/3 cup	75 mL
Pineapple juice	1/4 cup	60 mL
Lime juice	2 tbsp.	30 mL
Salt	1/4 tsp.	1 mL
Boneless, skinless chicken breast halves (4 – 6 oz., 113 – 170 g, each)	4	4
Cooking oil	1 tsp.	5 mL
Paprika	1/2 tsp.	2 mL
Seasoned salt	1/2 tsp.	2 mL
Pepper	1/4 tsp.	1 mL
Coconut rum	1/4 cup	60 mL
Brown sugar, packed	1 1/2 tbsp.	25 mL

In a blender or food processor, process first 6 ingredients until a thick paste forms.

Cut slits horizontally in chicken breasts to form pockets and fill with basil mixture. Secure with wooden picks.

Combine next 4 ingredients and rub over chicken.

Combine rum and brown sugar. Grill chicken on direct medium heat for 5 to 6 minutes per side, brushing occasionally with rum mixture, until chicken is no longer pink inside. Cover with foil and let stand for 5 minutes. Serves 4.

---

1 serving: 340 Calories; 13 g Total Fat (8 g Mono, 1 g Poly, 3.5 g Sat); 80 mg Cholesterol; 13 g Carbohydrate (2 g Fibre, 10 g Sugar); 34 g Protein; 450 mg Sodium

ABOUT PESTO

Pesto is an herb sauce that originated in the city of Genoa, in northwestern Italy. Traditionally a method of preserving herbs in oil, pesto has experienced an explosion in popularity in recent years. Traditional pesto is a simple blend of basil, olive oil, pine nuts (or walnuts) and garlic mashed up with a mortar and pestle; the addition of Parmesan or other hard cheeses is optional, and may not be advisable in pestos made from herbs other than basil.

Chicken Churrasco

Stuffed with a chimichurri paste of fresh parsley, oregano and garlic, this chicken will conjure up visions of an animated churrascaria. Let the revelry of this traditional Latin American barbecue house set the tone for your evening on the patio.

Chopped fresh parsley	1 cup	250 mL
Chopped fresh oregano	1/2 cup	125 mL
Olive oil	1/4 cup	60 mL
White wine vinegar	3 tbsp.	45 mL
Garlic cloves	6	6
Salt	2 tsp.	10 mL
Pepper	1 tsp.	5 mL
Whole chicken	4 lbs.	1.8 kg
Smoked sweet paprika	2 tsp.	10 mL

In a blender or food processor, process first 7 ingredients until smooth.

Cut along both sides of chicken backbone. Remove and discard backbone. Turn chicken over and press open. Carefully loosen skin but do not remove. Stuff parsley mixture between skin and meat, spreading mixture as evenly as possible. Rub paprika over surface of chicken. Chill, covered, for 4 hours. Prepare grill for direct high heat with a drip pan filled halfway with water. Place chicken, skin-side down, over drip pan. Place 2 foil-wrapped bricks directly on chicken (see Why To, below). Cook for about 5 minutes until dark grill marks appear. Turn off burner under chicken and cook for 30 minutes. Remove bricks and turn chicken over. Cook for about 45 minutes until internal temperature reaches 180°F (82°C). Serves 6.

---

1 serving: 270 Calories; 14 g Total Fat (8 g Mono, 2 g Poly, 2.5 g Sat); 102 mg Cholesterol; 3 g Carbohydrate (TRACE Fibre, 0 g Sugar); 32 g Protein; 900 mg Sodium

WHY TO
Weighing down the chicken with bricks while it's cooking helps grill marks to appear evenly on the skin.

ABOUT CHIMICHURRI AND CHURRASCO
Chimichurri is a garlicky sauce originating in Argentina. It usually accompanies grilled meats or is used as a meat marinade. Churrasco is a Spanish and Portuguese term referring to different cuts of beef or to grilled meat in general.

Mango Teriyaki-glazed Turkey

Explore the sweet creaminess of mango—first as a glaze for succulent turkey breasts, then as a grilled accompaniment, with smoky top notes to complement the main course.

Chopped mango (see Tip, below)	1/2 cup	125 mL
Soy sauce	1/2 cup	125 mL
Mirin	1/4 cup	60 mL
Sake	1/4 cup	60 mL
Brown sugar, packed	2 tbsp.	30 mL
Rice vinegar	2 tbsp.	30 mL
Ground ginger	3/4 tsp.	4 mL
Boneless, skinless turkey breast halves (about 12 oz., 340 g, each)	2	2
Salt, sprinkle		
Pepper, sprinkle		
Mangoes, peeled	2	2
Rice vinegar	2 tbsp.	30 mL
Brown sugar, packed	1 tbsp.	15 mL

In a blender or food processor, process first 7 ingredients until smooth. Transfer to a saucepan. Gently boil on medium, stirring occasionally, until thickened to a syrup consistency.

Sprinkle turkey with salt and pepper. Grill on direct medium heat for about 12 minutes per side, turning occasionally and brushing with mango mixture, until browned and internal temperature reaches 170°F (77°C). Cover with foil and let stand for 10 minutes. Cut turkey into thin slices.

Cut mangoes lengthwise around pit to create 4 grilling pieces (see How To, below). Combine rice vinegar and brown sugar. Brush over mango grilling pieces. Grill on direct medium heat for about 4 minutes per side. Cut crosswise into thin slices. Serve with turkey. Serves 6.

1 serving: 250 Calories; 1 g Total Fat (0 g Mono, 0 g Poly, 0 g Sat); 70 mg Cholesterol; 25 g Carbohydrate (2 g Fibre, 22 g Sugar); 31 g Protein; 1300 mg Sodium

HOW TO CUT MANGO
If using two whole mangoes, you should get four nice even pieces for grilling.

TIP
Cut any remaining mango flesh from around the pit and use in the glaze.

Sweet Spice Chicken with Smoky Rhubarb Barbecue Sauce

Tart rhubarb and the smoky heat of chipotle pepper bring gourmet flair to a simple barbecue sauce. Enjoy the sweetness of summer in style!

Chopped rhubarb	2 cups	500 mL
Dry red wine	1 cup	250 mL
Brown sugar, packed	1/2 cup	125 mL
Ketchup	1/2 cup	125 mL
Cinnamon sticks (4 inches, 10 cm, each)	2	2
Chopped chipotle pepper in adobo sauce (see Tip, page 36)	1 tsp.	5 mL
Salt	1/2 tsp.	2 mL
Brown sugar, packed	1 tbsp.	15 mL
Ground cinnamon	1 tsp.	5 mL
Ground ginger	1 tsp.	5 mL
Ground cloves	1/2 tsp.	2 mL
Salt	1/2 tsp.	2 mL
Boneless, skinless, chicken breast halves (4 – 6 oz., 113 – 170 g, each)	6	6

Combine first 7 ingredients in a saucepan. Gently boil on medium, stirring occasionally, until thickened and reduced by half. Remove and discard cinnamon sticks. Carefully process rhubarb mixture in blender or food processor until smooth (see Safety Tip, below).

Combine next 5 ingredients and rub over chicken. Grill on direct medium heat for about 7 minutes per side until internal temperature reaches 170°F (77°C). Serve with rhubarb mixture. Serves 6.

1 serving: 300 Calories; 2.5 g Total Fat (0 g Mono, 0 g Poly, 0 g Sat); 80 mg Cholesterol; 29 g Carbohydrate (1 g Fibre, 26 g Sugar); 33 g Protein; 750 mg Sodium

SAFETY TIP
Follow manufacturer's instructions for processing hot liquids.

Hoisin Five-spice Drumsticks

Mahogany hues entice the eye, while the distinctive flavours of Chinese five-spice powder appeal to the taste buds, creating memorable drumsticks to tempt the senses.

Hoisin sauce	1/3 cup	75 mL
Ketchup	1/4 cup	60 mL
Dry sherry	1 tbsp.	15 mL
Garlic powder	1 tsp.	5 mL
Chinese five-spice powder	2 tsp.	10 mL
Ground ginger	2 tsp.	10 mL
Chicken drumsticks (3 – 5 oz., 85 – 140 g, each), skin removed (see Tip, page 106)	12	12

Combine first 4 ingredients.

Combine five-spice powder and ginger. Sprinkle over drumsticks. Grill on direct medium heat for about 35 minutes, turning occasionally and brushing with hoisin mixture, until internal temperature reaches 170°F (77°C). Makes 12 drumsticks.

---

1 drumstick: 90 Calories; 3 g Total Fat (1 g Mono, 1 g Poly, 1 g Sat); 40 mg Cholesterol; 5 g Carbohydrate (0 g Fibre, 2 g Sugar); 11 g Protein; 230 mg Sodium

Brined Turkey with Orange Thyme Sauce

Although traditionally served in fall and winter, turkey can take centre stage in the middle of summer. Paired with colourful salads or grilled vegetables, this orange and thyme turkey is perfect for a backyard birthday or anniversary celebration.

Water	2 gallons	8 L
Salt	2 cups	500 mL
Can of frozen concentrated orange juice	12 1/2 oz.	355 mL
Whole turkey (not self-basting), giblets and neck removed	12 lbs.	5.4 kg
Large unpeeled orange, quartered	1	1
Fresh thyme sprigs	6	6
Olive oil	2 tbsp.	30 mL
Can of condensed chicken broth	10 oz.	284 mL
Ketchup	1 cup	250 mL
Frozen concentrated orange juice, thawed	1/2 cup	125 mL
Prepared mustard	1/4 cup	60 mL
Pepper	1/2 tsp.	2 mL
Chopped fresh thyme	1 tbsp.	15 mL

Stir first 3 ingredients until salt is dissolved. Place turkey in large stock pot or pail. Pour salt mixture over turkey and chill for 4 hours (see Tip, below). Drain and discard salt mixture. Rinse turkey inside and out under running water. Drain and pat dry with paper towels. Fold wings under body.

Place orange and thyme sprigs in cavity of turkey and rub skin with olive oil. Prepare grill for indirect medium heat with a drip pan. Cook turkey, breast-side down, for 1 hour. Turn and cook for 1 to 1 1/2 hours, rotating turkey 180° after 40 minutes, until meat thermometer inserted in thickest part of thigh reaches 165°F (74°C). Cover with foil and let stand for 15 minutes. Remove and discard orange and thyme sprigs.

Combine next 5 ingredients in a saucepan. Bring to a boil, stirring occasionally. Remove from heat and stir in thyme. Serve with turkey. Serves 12.

1 serving: 650 Calories; 29 g Total Fat (10 g Mono, 7 g Poly, 8 g Sat); 270 mg Cholesterol; 14 g Carbohydrate (0 g Fibre, 12 g Sugar); 79 g Protein; 1310 mg Sodium

TIP

This brine is extra salty, so it does its work in short order. If you have the time and space to brine the turkey overnight, reduce the salt by half.

Cumin Pork Chops with Corn Salsa

Lingering on the patio deck is easy when these cumin-scented pork chops are on the menu. The grill-kissed corn imparts a sweet, smoky flavour to the salsa.

Medium corncobs, in husk, soaked in water for 1 hour	3	3
Medium onion, cut into 1/2 inch (12 mm) slices	1	1
Medium red pepper	1	1
Medium tomatillos, papery husks removed	2	2
Balsamic vinegar	2 tbsp.	30 mL
Chopped fresh cilantro	2 tbsp.	30 mL
Lime juice	2 tbsp.	30 mL
Garlic clove, minced	1	1
Granulated sugar	1 tsp.	5 mL
Ground cumin	1/2 tsp.	2 mL
Olive oil	2 tbsp.	30 mL
Ground cumin	1 tsp.	5 mL
Salt	1/2 tsp.	2 mL
Pepper	1/2 tsp.	2 mL
Bone-in pork rib chops (about 1 inch, 2.5 cm, thick), trimmed of fat	4	4

Grill corncobs on direct medium heat for about 30 minutes, turning every 5 minutes, until lightly charred. Grill onion and red pepper for about 20 minutes, turning occasionally, until tender. Grill tomatillos for about 15 minutes, turning occasionally, until softened. Let stand until cool enough to handle. Cut corn kernels from cobs, dice onion and red pepper and chop tomatillos. Combine all vegetables in a medium bowl.

Add next 6 ingredients and toss. Let stand for 30 minutes to blend flavours. Makes about 3 1/2 cups (875 mL) salsa.

Combine next 4 ingredients and rub on pork chops. Chill for 30 minutes. Grill on direct medium heat for about 12 minutes per side until internal temperature reaches 160°F (71°C). Rotate meat 45° after 5 minutes to create attractive grill marks. Cover with foil and let stand for 5 minutes. Serve with corn salsa. Serves 4.

1 serving: 470 Calories; 29 g Total Fat (15 g Mono, 3.5 g Poly, 8 g Sat); 90 mg Cholesterol; 20 g Carbohydrate (4 g Fibre, 8 g Sugar); 33 g Protein; 370 mg Sodium

Runaway Five-spice Ribs

The complex aroma of garlic, herbs, spices and citrus. The sizzle of saucy ribs cooking on the grill. The tender meat pulling away from the bone. The succulent flavours playing on the palate. With all of its sensory appeal, this dish is a runaway hit.

Brown sugar, packed	1/4 cup	60 mL
Chopped fresh cilantro	1/4 cup	60 mL
Lime juice	1/4 cup	60 mL
Frozen concentrated orange juice, thawed	1/4 cup	60 mL
Soy sauce	1/4 cup	60 mL
Sesame oil	1 tbsp.	15 mL
Garlic cloves, minced	2	2
Chinese five-spice powder	1 tsp.	5 mL
Pepper	1/2 tsp.	2 mL
Racks of baby back ribs (about 1 lb., 454 g, each), see Tip, below	2	2

Combine first 9 ingredients in a 9 x 13 inch (23 x 33 cm) baking dish.

Add ribs and turn to coat. Chill, covered, for at least 6 hours or overnight. Drain marinade into a saucepan. Simmer on medium-low until thickened. Cook ribs on indirect medium heat for about 1 hour, turning occasionally, until meat is tender and starting to pull away from the bones. Cook for 30 to 45 minutes, turning often and brushing with marinade, until ribs are glazed. Cover with foil and let stand for 10 minutes. Cut into 3-bone portions. Makes about eight 3-bone portions.

3-bone portion: 390 Calories; 28 g Total Fat; (13 g Mono, 3 g Poly, 10 g Sat); 90 mg Cholesterol; 11 g Carbohydrate (0 g Fibre, 10 g Sugar); 20 g Protein; 550 mg Sodium

TIP
Before cooking ribs, wash them and peel away the membrane or "silver skin." If left on the meat, this membrane will toughen and prevent any seasonings from penetrating it while it cooks.

Herb and Pepper Steak

Hands-on preparation is always more fun with a full-textured rub. Feel the coarse grains of salt and pepper under the fingertips; appreciate the aroma of garlic and rosemary. Finally, revel in the flavours of this lovely steak.

Bone-in beef rib steaks (3/4 – 1 lb, 340 – 454 g, each), about 1 inch (2.5 cm) thick	2	2
Cooking oil	2 tsp.	10 mL
Coarsely ground pepper	2 tbsp.	30 mL
Coarse sea salt	2 tsp.	10 mL
Dried rosemary, crushed	2 tsp.	10 mL
Garlic powder	2 tsp.	10 mL
Dried basil	1 tsp.	5 mL
Dried oregano	1 tsp.	5 mL
Dried thyme	1 tsp.	5 mL
Ground coriander	3/4 tsp.	4 mL
Cayenne pepper	1/4 tsp.	1 mL

Rub steaks with cooking oil.

Combine remaining 9 ingredients and rub over steaks. Chill for 10 minutes. Grill on direct medium-high heat for about 8 minutes per side for medium-rare or until steak reaches desired doneness. Cover with foil and let stand for 10 minutes. Serves 4.

1 serving: 310 Calories; 14 g Total Fat (6 g Mono, 1 g Poly, 4.5 g Sat); 80 mg Cholesterol; 4 g Carbohydrate (1 g Fibre, 0 g Sugar); 38 g Protein; 1180 mg Sodium

ABOUT STEAKS
Buying a good steak for the barbecue can be confusing; often different names are applied to the same cut of meat. It helps to divide steaks into two broad categories: steaks that can be put straight on the grill and those which benefit from marinating to increase tenderness. Steaks that are "grill-ready" include rib, rib-eye, strip loin, T-bone, tenderloin and top sirloin. "Marinating" steaks include eye of round, flank, full round, inside round, outside round and sirloin tip.

Lamb Chops with Hazelnut Gremolata

Finger food with a touch of decadence—a hazelnut coating adds crunch and interest to these well-dressed chops.

Chopped fresh parsley	1/4 cup	60 mL
Chopped sliced hazelnuts, toasted (see How To, below)	2 tbsp.	30 mL
Garlic cloves, minced	2	2
Grated lemon zest	2 tsp.	10 mL
Salt	1/4 tsp.	1 mL
Balsamic vinegar	2 tbsp.	30 mL
Extra-virgin olive oil	2 tbsp.	30 mL
Salt, sprinkle		
Coarsely ground pepper, sprinkle		
Racks of lamb (8 ribs each), about 1 1/3 lbs., (625 g), separated into 16 chops	2	2

Combine first 5 ingredients.

Combine next 4 ingredients and brush over lamb chops. Grill on direct medium heat for about 2 minutes per side until internal temperature reaches 145°F (63°C) for medium-rare or until lamb reaches desired doneness. Sprinkle with hazelnut mixture. Makes 16 lamb chops.

---

1 lamb chop: 305 Calories; 28 g Total Fat (12 g Mono, 2.5 g Poly, 11 g Sat); 57 mg Cholesterol; 1 g Carbohydrate (0 g Fibre, 0 g Sugar); 11 g Protein; 80 mg Sodium

HOW TO TOAST NUTS
Toasting nuts brings out an aroma and depth of flavour not apparent in the raw product. To toast nuts, seeds or coconut, put them into an ungreased frying pan. Heat on medium for 3 to 5 minutes, stirring often, until golden. To bake, spread them evenly in an ungreased shallow pan. Bake in 350°F (175°C) oven for 5 to 10 minutes, stirring or shaking often, until golden.

ABOUT GREMOLATA
This anglicized version of the Italian word *gremolada* is used to describe an aromatic mixture, usually of lemon zest, garlic and parsley, that is sprinkled over meat at the end of its cooking time.

Chili Cherry Beef Ribs

Sweet cherry blends with chili warmth for a full-bodied sauce that will have your dining companions begging for your secret. Life really is a bowl full of cherries!

Cherry jam	1 cup	250 mL
Hickory barbecue sauce	1/3 cup	75 mL
Chili paste (sambal oelek)	1 tbsp.	15 mL
Racks of beef back ribs (2 – 3 lbs, 900 g – 1.4 kg, each), trimmed of fat	2	2
Seasoned salt	1 tbsp.	15 mL

Combine first 3 ingredients in a saucepan. Gently boil on medium for 5 minutes to blend flavours.

Rub ribs with seasoned salt. Prepare grill for indirect medium heat with a drip pan. Cook ribs, meat-side down, for 1 hour. Turn and cook for about 1 hour, brushing occasionally with cherry mixture, until meat is tender, glazed and pulling away from bones. Cover with foil and let stand for 10 minutes. Cut into 1-bone portions. Makes about 14 ribs.

---

1 rib: 490 Calories; 38 g Total Fat (16 g Mono, 1.5 g Poly, 16 g Sat); 95 mg Cholesterol; 17 g Carbohydrate (0 g Fibre, 14 g Sugar); 21 g Protein; 500 mg Sodium

ABOUT SAMBAL OELEK

This much-used condiment is popular in Indonesia, Malaysia and India and is made primarily of chilies, brown sugar and salt.

Orange Chili-stuffed Pork Chops

Duelling sources of heat play off the tongue with these Italian sausage-stuffed pork chops. Add the smoke from the apple wood chips and the sweetness of the glaze for a meaty, flavourful experience.

Cooking oil	2 tsp.	10 mL
Hot Italian sausage, casing removed	3/4 lb.	340 g
Chopped onion	1 cup	250 mL
Garlic cloves, minced	2	2
Diced red pepper	1/2 cup	125 mL
Bone-in pork rib chops (about 1 1/2 inches, 3.8 cm, thick), trimmed of fat (see Tip, below)	4	4
Salt, sprinkle		
Pepper, sprinkle		
Sweet chili sauce	1/2 cup	125 mL
Grated orange zest	2 tsp.	10 mL
Apple wood chips, soaked in water for 1 hour and drained	2 cups	500 mL

Heat cooking oil in a frying pan on medium high. Add next 3 ingredients and scramble-fry until sausage is no longer pink.

Add red pepper and scramble-fry until tender-crisp. Remove pan from heat and let stand until cool.

Cut slits horizontally in pork chops to create pockets. Fill with sausage mixture and secure with wooden picks. Sprinkle with salt and pepper.

Combine chili sauce and orange zest.

Put wood chips into smoker box. Prepare grill for indirect medium heat with smoker box. Cook pork chops for about 25 minutes per side, brushing occasionally with chili sauce mixture, until internal temperature of pork reaches 160°F (71°C). Cover with foil and let stand for 5 minutes. Remove picks before serving. Makes 4 stuffed pork chops.

---

1 stuffed pork chop: 640 Calories; 39 g Total Fat (18 g Mono, 4.5 g Poly, 13 g Sat); 160 mg Cholesterol; 20 g Carbohydrate (1 g Fibre, 15 g Sugar); 49 g Protein; 1140 mg Sodium

TIP
To find chops that are the required thickness, you may have to make a special request of your butcher.

MAKE AHEAD
The filling can be made a day ahead, but the chops should be stuffed just before they are cooked.

Tropical T-bone Steaks with Papaya Relish

Bring on the exotic with pineapple juice and papaya, chilled for contrast to the sizzling steaks. Why fly to the tropics when treats such as these can be conjured up on your own grill?

Large onion, cut crosswise into 1/2 inch (12 mm) slices	1	1
Small firm papayas, peeled and cut into 1/2 inch (12 mm) slices	2	2
Chopped fresh cilantro	2 tbsp.	30 mL
Pineapple juice	2 tbsp.	30 mL
White wine vinegar	2 tbsp.	30 mL
Brown sugar, packed	1 tbsp.	15 mL
Pineapple juice	1/2 cup	125 mL
Brown sugar, packed	2 tbsp.	30 mL
Soy sauce	2 tbsp.	30 mL
White wine vinegar	1 tbsp.	15 mL
Finely grated ginger root	2 tsp.	10 mL
Garlic cloves, minced	2	2
T-bone steaks (about 3/4 lb., 340 g, each), about 3/4 inch (2 cm) thick	2	2

Grill onion on direct medium heat for about 20 minutes, turning occasionally, until tender.

Cook papaya for 2 to 3 minutes per side until grill marks appear. Let stand until cool enough to handle. Chop onion and papaya.

Whisk next 4 ingredients together until brown sugar is dissolved. Toss with onion and papaya. Chill.

Combine next 6 ingredients. Pour into a large resealable freezer bag, reserving 2 tbsp. (30 mL). Add steaks and chill for 1 hour. Drain and discard marinade. Blot steaks dry and grill on direct medium-high heat, brushing with reserved pineapple juice mixture, for about 5 minutes per side for medium-rare or until steak reaches desired doneness. Serve with papaya mixture. Serves 4.

---

1 serving: 330 Calories; 8 g Total Fat (3.5 g Mono, 0.5 g Poly, 3 g Sat); 65 mg Cholesterol; 26 g Carbohydrate (2 g Fibre, 14 g Sugar); 38 g Protein; 570 mg Sodium

TIP
Fresh pineapple and papaya contain enzymes known to tenderize meat quite quickly without altering the meat's flavour very much. Next time you need some natural meat tenderizers, consider adding fresh pineapple and papaya to your marinade.

Curry Coconut Ribs

Creaminess, tangy freshness and chili heat combine with tender, fall-off-the-bone pork for a sumptuous update to traditional barbecued ribs.

Racks of pork side ribs (about 1 1/2 lbs., 680 g, each), trimmed of fat	2	2
Garlic cloves, sliced	5	5
Ginger root slices (1/4 inch, 6 mm, thick)	4	4
Seasoned salt	1 tbsp.	15 mL
Cooking oil	1/2 tsp.	2 mL
Red curry paste	1 tbsp.	15 mL
Can of coconut milk	14 oz.	398 mL
Brown sugar, packed	3 tbsp.	45 mL
Soy sauce	3 tbsp.	45 mL
Lime juice	2 tbsp.	30 mL

Cut each rack of ribs in half.

Combine next 3 ingredients and ribs in a Dutch oven or large pot. Add water to cover and bring to a boil. Simmer, covered, on medium-low for about 1 hour until ribs are tender. Drain, discarding garlic and ginger. Transfer ribs to a 9 x 13 inch (23 x 33 cm) baking dish.

Heat cooking oil in a saucepan on medium and add curry paste. Heat and stir for about 1 minute until curry is fragrant.

Add remaining 4 ingredients. Simmer, uncovered, for 10 minutes to blend flavours. Pour over ribs and turn to coat. Let stand for 30 minutes. Grill ribs on direct medium heat for about 15 minutes, turning often and brushing with curry mixture until ribs are glazed and heated through. Cut into 2-bone portions. Makes about twelve 2-bone portions.

2-bone portion: 410 Calories; 34 g Total Fat (12 g Mono, 25 g Poly, 16 g Sat); 90 mg Cholesterol; 5 g Carbohydrate (0 g Fibre, 3 g Sugar); 21 g Protein; 370 mg Sodium

MAKE AHEAD
Cook the ribs and marinate in the refrigerator for up to a day in advance.

Mole-Ole! Steak with Chili Salsa

We've captured the essence of a typical mole in this savoury rub. Let the scent of cinnamon, cocoa and chipotle chilies transport you to your favourite Mexican cantina.

Brown sugar, packed	1 tbsp.	15 mL
Cocoa powder, sifted if lumpy	1 tbsp.	15 mL
Ground chipotle chili pepper	1 tbsp.	15 mL
Dried oregano	2 tsp.	10 mL
Garlic powder	2 tsp.	10 mL
Ground cinnamon	1 tsp.	5 mL
Pepper	1 tsp.	5 mL
Diced tomato	1 cup	250 mL
Can of diced green chilies	4 oz.	113 g
Diced red onion	1/4 cup	60 mL
Chopped fresh cilantro	1 tbsp.	15 mL
Lime juice	1 tbsp.	15 mL
Cooking oil	1 tbsp.	15 mL
Beef strip loin steaks (about 6 oz., 170 g, each), about 3/4 inch (2 cm) thick	4	4

Coarse salt, sprinkle

Combine first 7 ingredients.

Combine next 5 ingredients and stir in 2 tsp. (10 mL) of cocoa mixture. Let stand for 30 minutes.

Stir cooking oil into remaining cocoa mixture until smooth. Rub over steaks and chill, covered, for 30 minutes. Grill on direct medium-high heat for about 5 minutes per side for medium-rare or until steaks reach desired doneness. Cover with foil and let stand for 10 minutes.

Sprinkle steaks and tomato mixture with salt. Serves 4.

---

1 serving: 370 Calories; 15 g Total Fat (7 g Mono, 1.5 g Poly, 4.5 g Sat); 95 mg Cholesterol; 11 g Carbohydrate (3 g Fibre, 6 g Sugar); 47 g Protein; 240 mg Sodium

ABOUT MOLE
This savoury sauce of Mexican origin incorporates a small amount of chocolate or cocoa. Although it may seem odd to have chocolate in a savoury sauce, chocolate adds a rich colour and depth of flavour rather than sweetness and goes very well with poultry or beef.

Bourbon Street Steak with Citrus Butter

A dash of the French Quarter adds flair to your dinner. A zesty citrus butter complements the Cajun-spiced steak—all you need is a little New Orleans jazz playing in the background.

Bourbon	1/2 cup	125 mL
Minced onion	2 tbsp.	30 mL
Butter, softened	1/4 cup	60 mL
Chopped fresh chives	1 tbsp.	15 mL
Chopped fresh thyme	1/2 tsp.	2 mL
Grated lemon zest	1/2 tsp.	2 mL
Grated orange zest	1/2 tsp.	2 mL
Brown sugar, packed	1 tbsp.	15 mL
Onion powder	1 tbsp.	15 mL
Smoked sweet paprika	1 tbsp.	15 mL
Salt	2 tsp.	10 mL
Dried thyme	1 1/2 tsp.	7 mL
Garlic powder	1 1/2 tsp.	7 mL
Chili powder	1/2 tsp.	2 mL
Pepper	1/2 tsp.	2 mL
Cayenne pepper	1/4 tsp.	1 mL
Beef strip loin steaks (about 6 oz., 170 g, each), about 3/4 inch (2 cm) thick	4	4

Combine bourbon and onion in a frying pan. Cook on medium for about 5 minutes until liquid is almost all evaporated. Remove from heat, leaving onion in pan to cool completely.

Stir in next 5 ingredients and spoon onto a sheet of waxed paper. Form into a 3 inch (7.5 cm) long cylinder. Wrap tightly and freeze for about 1 hour until firm (see How To, page 84).

Combine next 9 ingredients and rub over steaks. Grill on direct medium-high heat for about 5 minutes per side for medium-rare or until steak reaches desired doneness. Cover with foil and let stand for 10 minutes. Serve with sliced citrus butter medallions. Serves 4.

---

1 serving: 500 Calories; 23 g Total Fat (8 g Mono, 1 g Poly, 1 g Sat); 125 mg Cholesterol; 8 g Carbohydrate (1 g Fibre, 5 g Sugar); 46 g Protein; 1380 mg Sodium

Miso-glazed Pork Chops with Wasabi Mayonnaise

Explore the tastes of Japan with these moist pork chops accentuated with a miso-sesame glaze. The mayonnaise accompaniment offers just enough of a kick to make your guests take notice—and seconds!

Mayonnaise	1/2 cup	125 mL
Mirin	2 tsp.	10 mL
Wasabi paste	2 tsp.	10 mL
Finely grated ginger root	1 tsp.	5 mL
White miso	1/4 cup	60 mL
Brown sugar, packed	3 tbsp.	45 mL
Mirin	2 tbsp.	30 mL
Sake	2 tbsp.	30 mL
Tahini	2 tbsp.	30 mL
Soy sauce	2 tsp.	10 mL
Bone-in pork chops, trimmed of fat	4	4

Combine first 4 ingredients. Chill for 30 minutes to blend flavours.

Combine next 6 ingredients and brush on both sides of pork chops. Grill on direct medium-high heat for about 5 minutes per side, brushing occasionally with remaining miso mixture, until internal temperature reaches 160°F (71°C). Serve with mayonnaise mixture. Serves 4.

---

1 serving: 500 Calories; 30 g Total Fat (15 g Mono, 7 g Poly, 4.5 g Sat); 55 mg Cholesterol; 25 g Carbohydrate (2 g Fibre, 17 g Sugar); 23 g Protein; 1060 mg Sodium

ABOUT PORK

Years ago, pork was a fatty meat, but modern pork is very lean. It is essential not to overcook it, or it will be dry and tough.

Jamaican Flank Steak

The classic seasonings of Jamaican jerk infuse an ordinary steak with extraordinary flavour. A few paper lanterns and some rum-based drinks and you're well on your way to a Caribbean evening.

Jerk seasoning paste	3 tbsp.	45 mL
Balsamic vinegar	1 tbsp.	15 mL
Brown sugar, packed	1 tbsp.	15 mL
Tomato paste (see Tip, below)	1 tbsp.	15 mL
Dried thyme	1/4 tsp.	1 mL
Flank steak	1 1/2 lbs.	680 g

Combine first 5 ingredients and spread on both sides of steak. Chill, covered, for 1 hour. Grill on direct medium-high heat for about 5 minutes per side for medium-rare or until steak reaches desired doneness. Cover with foil and let stand for 10 minutes. Cut steak diagonally, across the grain, into very thin slices (see Why To, below). Serves 6.

1 serving: 210 Calories; 9 g Total Fat (3.5 g Mono, 0 g Poly, 3.5 g Sat); 45 mg Cholesterol; 6 g Carbohydrate (0 g Fibre, 5 g Sugar); 24 g Protein; 175 mg Sodium

TIP

If a recipe calls for less than an entire can of tomato paste, freeze the unopened can for 30 minutes. Open both ends and push the contents through one end. Slice off only what you need and freeze the remaining paste in a resealable freezer bag or plastic wrap for future use.

WHY TO

Cutting steak diagonally across the grain maximizes the meat's tenderness.

Moroccan Lamb Shanks

Pour orange blossom-scented water on your guests' hands just before eating to set the mood for an exotic Arabian feast.

Red wine	2/3 cup	150 mL
Medium onions, cut into 1/4 inch (6 mm) slices	2	2
Cinnamon sticks	2	2
Salt	1/2 tsp.	2 mL
Apricot jam	2 tbsp.	30 mL
Garlic cloves, minced	6	6
Ground cumin	1 tbsp.	15 mL
Ketchup	1 tbsp.	15 mL
Ground cinnamon	2 tsp.	10 mL
Salt	1 tsp.	5 mL
Pepper	1/2 tsp.	2 mL
Lamb shanks (about 3/4 lb., 340 g, each)	6	6

Combine first 4 ingredients in a greased 9 x 13 inch (23 x 33 cm) foil pan.

Combine next 7 ingredients and spread over lamb shanks. Sear on direct medium-high heat for about 8 minutes, turning every 2 to 3 minutes, until browned. Arrange lamb over onion mixture and cover tightly with foil. Cook on direct medium-high heat for 10 minutes, then turn off burner under pan, leaving opposite burner on. Cook for about 3 hours, rotating pan 180° every hour, until lamb is fork-tender (see Tip, below). Transfer lamb to serving plate and cover to keep warm. Remove and discard cinnamon sticks. Skim and discard fat from pan. In a blender or food processor, carefully process onion mixture until smooth (see Safety Tip, below). Serve with lamb. Serves 6.

---

1 serving: 480 Calories; 14 g Total Fat (6 g Mono, 1.5 g Poly, 5 g Sat); 220 mg Cholesterol; 8 g Carbohydrate (TRACE Fibre, 5 g Sugar); 70 g Protein; 830 mg Sodium

TIP
Lower cuts like veal osso bucco, pork hocks and lamb shanks have the toughest meat and the richest flavours. The collagen in the meat will melt at about 170°F (77°C), turning the meat from tough to tender. Be sure not to undercook these cuts. The wonderful aromatic smells may make it hard to resist, but your patience will be rewarded with succulent meat that falls right off the bone. Don't waste lamb shanks on those who like lamb just a little; save this recipe for those who love it!

SAFETY TIP
Follow manufacturer's instructions for processing hot liquids.

Porcini-rubbed Beef Roast

Roast beef seasoned with a rub of herbs, sea salt and dried porcini mushrooms turns any meal into a celebration, especially if paired with a horseradish and roasted garlic sauce.

Package of dried porcini mushrooms	3/4 oz.	22 g
Dried thyme	2 tsp.	10 mL
Dried rosemary, crushed	1 tsp.	5 mL
Coarse sea salt	1/2 tsp.	2 mL
Beef sirloin tip roast	4 1/2 lbs.	2 kg
Fresh white mushroom caps	12	12
Olive oil	2 tsp.	10 mL
Sour cream	1 cup	250 mL
Roasted garlic bulb (see How To, below), mashed	1	1
Prepared horseradish	1 tbsp.	15 mL
Lemon juice	2 tsp.	10 mL
Salt	1/2 tsp.	2 mL
Pepper	1/4 tsp.	1 mL

In a blender or food processor, process first 4 ingredients into a fine powder. Rub over entire surface of roast and chill, covered, for at least 6 hours or overnight. Set up roast on rotisserie and cook on direct medium heat for about 30 minutes until starting to brown. Reduce heat to medium-low. Cook for about 1 hour until internal temperature reaches 160°F (71°C) for medium or until roast reaches desired doneness. Remove from rotisserie. Cover with foil and let stand for 15 minutes before slicing.

Brush mushroom caps with olive oil. Grill on direct medium heat until golden.

Combine remaining 6 ingredients. Serve with roast and mushrooms. Serves 12.

---

1 serving: 260 Calories; 13 g Total Fat (5 g Mono, 0.5 g Poly, 5 g Sat); 72 mg Cholesterol; 3 g Carbohydrate (1 g Fibre, 0 g Sugar); 31 g Protein; 270 mg Sodium

HOW TO ROAST GARLIC

To roast garlic, trim 1/4 inch (6 mm) from each bulb to expose tops of cloves, leaving bulbs intact. Wrap bulbs individually in greased foil. Prepare grill for indirect medium heat. Cook for 30–45 minutes or until soft. Let stand until cool enough to handle. Squeeze garlic bulb to remove cloves from skins. Excess roasted garlic can be wrapped and stored in the freezer. To roast garlic in the oven, prepare as above and bake at 350°F (175°C) for about 45 minutes.

Meatloaf with Chipotle Ketchup

Invite good friends to share comfort food with Southwest flair. Smoked jalapeño peppers add a fiery twist to the ketchup for everyone's favourite meatloaf, making the possibility of leftovers nonexistent.

Jar of roasted red peppers, drained and chopped (see Tip, below)	12 oz.	340 mL
Brown sugar, packed	1/4 cup	60 mL
Orange juice	1/4 cup	60 mL
Cider vinegar	3 tbsp.	45 mL
Chopped chipotle pepper in adobo sauce (see Tip, page 36)	2 tsp.	10 mL
Salt	1/2 tsp.	2 mL
Large egg, fork-beaten	1	1
Fine dry bread crumbs	1 cup	250 mL
Milk	1/4 cup	60 mL
Montreal steak spice	1 tbsp.	15 mL
Worcestershire sauce	2 tsp.	10 mL
Lean ground beef	1 lb.	454 g
Lean ground pork	1 lb.	454 g

Combine first 6 ingredients in a saucepan. Bring to a boil. Simmer, partially covered, on medium-low for 15 minutes to blend flavours. In a blender or food processor, carefully process until smooth (see Safety Tip, below). Reserve 2/3 cup (150 mL).

Combine remaining 7 ingredients. Form into a 9 x 4 inch (23 x 10 cm) loaf in the centre of a greased foil pan. Cook meatloaf on indirect medium heat for 1 hour. Brush with remaining red pepper mixture and cook for about 15 minutes until internal temperature reaches 160°F (71°C). Cover with foil and let stand for 10 minutes. Cut into 1/2 inch (12 mm) thick slices. Transfer to a serving plate and serve with reserved red pepper mixture. Serves 8.

---

1 serving: 415 Calories; 21 g Total Fat (9.5 g Mono, 1.5 g Poly, 8 g Sat); 98 mg Cholesterol; 26 g Carbohydrate (TRACE Fibre, 8 g Sugar); 25 g Protein; 1060 mg Sodium

TIP
Instead of buying jarred peppers, you can roast red peppers easily in the oven, under the broiler or on the grill. For all three methods, cook the peppers until they are soft and the skin is quite charred. Cool, covered with foil, then peel and seed.

SAFETY TIP
Follow manufacturer's instructions for blending hot liquids.

Raspberry Balsamic Cornish Hens

Stuffed with lemon zest and Italian seasonings and basted with a raspberry-balsamic sauce, these small birds boast enormous flavour.

Butter, softened	1/4 cup	60 mL
Italian seasoning	2 tbsp.	30 mL
Grated lemon zest	2 tsp.	10 mL
Salt	1 tsp.	5 mL
Cornish hens (about 1 1/2 lbs., 680 g, each)	2	2
Seedless raspberry jam	1/2 cup	125 mL
Balsamic vinegar	1/4 cup	60 mL
Lemon juice	1 tbsp.	15 mL

Combine first 4 ingredients.

Carefully loosen skin on hens, but do not remove. Stuff butter mixture between skin and meat, spreading mixture as evenly as possible (see Why To, below). Chill, covered, for 30 minutes.

Combine remaining 3 ingredients in a saucepan. Gently boil on medium until thickened. Prepare grill for indirect medium heat with a drip pan. Cook hens, breast-side down, for 20 minutes. Turn. Cook for 30 to 40 minutes, brushing occasionally with jam mixture, until meat thermometer inserted in thickest part of breast reaches 180°F (82°C). Cover with foil and let stand for 10 minutes. Cut hens in half to serve. Serves 4.

---

1 serving: 550 Calories; 35 g Total Fat (13 g Mono, 5 g Poly, 14 g Sat); 200 mg Cholesterol; 29 g Carbohydrate (0 g Fibre, 26 g Sugar); 29 g Protein; 770 mg Sodium

WHY TO
Inserting the butter between the meat and the skin will help keep the hens moist and flavourful.

Cocoa-crusted Tenderloin with Stilton Crumble

An elegant entree seasoned with a touch of the unpredictable—cocoa and stilton—this tenderloin demands fine china and candlelight at any time of year. Match it with your favourite full-bodied red wine.

Beef tenderloin roast (see Tip, below)	2 1/2 lbs.	1.1 kg
Olive oil	2 tbsp.	30 mL
Brown sugar, packed	2 tbsp.	30 mL
Coarsely ground pepper	2 tbsp.	30 mL
Cocoa, sifted if lumpy	2 tbsp.	30 mL
Smoked sweet paprika	2 tbsp.	30 mL
Salt	1 1/4 tsp.	6 mL
Stilton cheese, crumbled	2 oz.	57 g

Rub entire surface of roast with olive oil. Combine next 5 ingredients and rub over roast. Prepare grill for indirect medium-high heat with a drip pan. Cook for 30 minutes, then rotate roast 180°. Cook for about 30 minutes until internal temperature reaches 145°F (63°C) for medium-rare or until roast reaches desired doneness. Cover with foil and let stand for 15 minutes. Cut roast into 1/2 inch (12 mm) thick slices.

Sprinkle with cheese. Serves 8.

1 serving: 240 Calories; 13.5 g Total Fat (6 g Mono, 0.5 g Poly, 5 g Sat); 59 mg Cholesterol; 5 g Carbohydrate (1 g Fibre, 3 g Sugar); 24 g Protein; 512 mg Sodium

TIP
If you can, get a tenderloin roast cut from the centre of the loin for an even-shaped roast.

ABOUT PAPRIKA
A spice most closely associated with Hungary and Hungarian cuisine (think chicken paprikash), paprika is also used extensively to flavour and colour Spanish, Portuguese, Turkish and Indian dishes. Paprika is divided into several categories depending on level of spiciness and colour, but the most common variety is derived from dried sweet red peppers and is known as sweet paprika.

Lemon Pistachio Pork

Crusted with pepper and stuffed with a sweet dried fruit and pistachio filling, this roast needs little attention once it's on the grill, leaving you free to spoil yourself with some down time before dinner.

Liquid honey	1/3 cup	75 mL
Lemon juice	3 tbsp.	45 mL
Finely grated ginger root	1 tbsp.	15 mL
Grated lemon zest (see Tip, page 98)	2 tsp.	10 mL
Ground cinnamon	1/2 tsp.	2 mL
Coarsely chopped roasted pistachios	1 cup	250 mL
Fine dry bread crumbs	1 cup	250 mL
Dark raisins	1/3 cup	75 mL
Dried cranberries	1/3 cup	75 mL
Boneless pork rib roast, frozen for 30 minutes (see Why To, below)	2 – 3 lbs.	900 g – 1.4 kg
Olive oil	2 tsp.	10 mL
Coarsely ground pepper	3 tbsp.	45 mL
Smoked sweet paprika	1 tbsp.	15 mL
Seasoned salt	1 1/2 tsp.	7 mL

Combine first 5 ingredients.

Add next 4 ingredients and stir until combined.

Place roast, fat-side up, on a cutting board. Using a sharp knife, cut horizontally, about 1/2 inch (12 mm) from bottom, almost, but not quite, through to other side (see How To, below). Open roast like a book and cut through thicker half of roast, about 1/2 inch (12 mm) from bottom, almost, but not quite, through to other side. Repeat, if necessary, until roast is an even 1/2 inch (12 mm) thickness. Spread pistachio mixture over roast, leaving a 1/2 inch (12 mm) border. Roll up tightly from short edge to enclose. Tie with butcher's string at 1 inch (2.5 cm) intervals.

Brush entire surface of roast with olive oil. Combine remaining 3 ingredients and sprinkle over roast. Prepare grill for indirect medium heat with a drip pan. Cook roast, fat-side up, for about 1 1/2 hours, turning once, until internal temperature of pork reaches at least 140°F (60°C) or until desired doneness. Cover with foil and let stand for 15 minutes. Remove string and cut into 1/2 inch (12 mm) thick slices. Serves 8.

1 serving: 450 Calories; 18 g Total Fat (8 g Mono, 3.5 g Poly, 4.5 g Sat); 80 mg Cholesterol; 37 g Carbohydrate (4 g Fibre, 21 g Sugar); 36 g Protein; 450 mg Sodium

WHY TO
Partially freezing the roast will help it retain its shape while cutting.

HOW TO CUT ROAST

Rosemary Plum Leg of Lamb

Exotic spices and luscious summer plums meld as the lamb roasts slowly on the grill. The aromas will entice neighbours to appear at your gate bearing bottles of shiraz.

Cans of prune plums, drained and pitted (14 oz., 398 mL, each)	3	3
Plum jam	1/2 cup	125 mL
Balsamic vinegar	2 tbsp.	30 mL
Brown sugar, packed	2 tbsp.	30 mL
Fresh rosemary, chopped	2 tbsp.	30 mL
Finely grated ginger root	1 tbsp.	15 mL
Ground cinnamon	1 1/2 tsp.	7 mL
Salt	1/2 tsp.	2 mL
Ground cardamom	1/4 tsp.	1 mL
Ground cloves	1/8 tsp.	0.5 mL
Boneless leg of lamb roast (see Tip, below)	3 1/2 – 4 lbs.	1.6 – 1.8 kg

In a blender or food processor, process first 10 ingredients until smooth. Reserve 2 cups (500 mL).

Prepare grill for indirect medium heat with a drip pan. Cook roast for 1 hour. Turn and cook for about 1 hour, brushing often with plum sauce, until internal temperature reaches 145°F (63°C) for medium-rare or until roast reaches desired doneness. Cover with foil and let stand for 15 minutes. Cut roast into slices. Warm reserved plum sauce and serve with roast. Serves 10.

---

1 serving: 340 Calories; 7 g Total Fat (2.5 g Mono, 0 g Poly, 3 g Sat); 125 mg Cholesterol; 34 g Carbohydrate (1 g Fibre, 29 g Sugar); 36 g Protein; 200 mg Sodium

TIP

Ask your butcher to completely de-bone, tie and trim the lamb roast for you.

ABOUT LAMB

If butchered before it's one year old, sheep meat is called lamb. After, it's known as mutton and has a stronger flavour.

Port-glazed Pork Tenderloin with Stilton Pears

The tantalizing choice is yours: green-skinned pears pair well visually with the fresh chives, while red-skinned pears play off the redcurrant jelly and ruby port. Either way, the result is fabulous!

Redcurrant jelly	1/2 cup	125 mL
Ruby port	1/2 cup	125 mL
Ground ginger	1/2 tsp.	2 mL
Salt	1/2 tsp.	2 mL
Pepper	1/2 tsp.	2 mL
Ground cloves	1/8 tsp.	0.5 mL
Pork tenderloin, trimmed of fat	1 lb.	454 g
Salt, sprinkle		
Pepper, sprinkle		
Firm medium unpeeled pears, cored and halved	2	2
Cooking oil	1 tsp.	5 mL
Stilton cheese	4 oz.	113 g

Combine first 6 ingredients in a saucepan. Gently boil on medium, stirring occasionally, until reduced and thickened. Remove from heat and let stand until cool. Reserve 1/4 cup (60 mL).

Sprinkle tenderloin with salt and pepper. Grill on direct medium-high heat for about 25 minutes, turning often and brushing with reserved glaze during final 5 minutes of cooking, until internal temperature reaches 160°F (71°C). Cover with foil and let stand for 5 minutes. Cut diagonally into 12 slices.

Brush cut-sides of pears with cooking oil. Grill pears, cut-side down, on direct medium-high heat for about 4 minutes. Rotate pears 45° after 2 minutes to create attractive grill marks. Turn pears cut-side up and top with cheese. Cook for about 2 minutes until cheese is softened. Serve with tenderloin and remaining glaze. Serves 4.

---

1 serving: 460 Calories; 16 g Total Fat (6 g Mono, 1 g Poly, 8 g Sat); 95 mg Cholesterol; 44 g Carbohydrate (3 g Fibre, 35 g Sugar); 30 g Protein; 750 mg Sodium

ABOUT PORK TENDERLOIN

Pork tenderloin is low in fat and small in size, so it can be cooked quickly. It is a good meat for grilling for this reason. Because it has little fat, it is not as robustly flavoured as some other cuts of pork, so it goes well with stronger-tasting ingredients for more depth of flavour.

Dijon Prime Rib

For decadence, few things match a prime rib. The barbecue adds a distinctive smokiness to the roast, and the garlic cloves roast while cooking, infusing the meat with fabulous flavour.

Bone-in prime rib roast (see Tip, below)	6 lbs.	2.7 kg
Garlic cloves, halved lengthwise	4	4
Dijon mustard (with whole seeds)	1/3 cup	75 mL
Mayonnaise	3 tbsp.	45 mL
Prepared horseradish	2 tbsp.	30 mL
Liquid honey	1 tsp.	5 mL
Salt	1 tsp.	5 mL
Coarsely ground pepper	1 tsp.	5 mL

Cut 8 slits randomly in roast with a small, sharp knife. Push garlic clove halves halfway into each slit.

Combine remaining 6 ingredients. Spoon over roast, spreading evenly over top and sides. Prepare grill for indirect medium heat with a drip pan. Cook, bone-side down, for 1 hour, then rotate roast 180°. Cook for about 1 1/2 hours until internal temperature reaches 145°F (63°C) for medium-rare or until roast reaches desired doneness. Cover with foil and let stand for 15 minutes (see Why To, below). Cut roast into slices. Serves 12.

---

1 serving: 690 Calories; 57 g Total Fat (25 g Mono, 2.5 g Poly, 23 g Sat); 160 mg Cholesterol; 2 g Carbohydrate (0 g Fibre, TRACE Sugar); 38 g Protein; 440 mg Sodium

TIP
When you purchase the roast, have the butcher cut off the ribs then tie them back in place. While the meat is roasting, it will take on the delicious flavour of the bones, but they can be removed easily from the roast just before carving.

WHY TO
Be sure to let roasts rest for 15 to 30 minutes after coming off the barbecue (the bigger the roast, the longer the stand time). Letting it stand will give the meat a chance to finish cooking (it will come up several degrees) and the juices will be reabsorbed into the meat, making your roast more moist and succulent.

In the Cooler

Nothing beats a smooth, ice-cold brew to go with something hot off the grill. Choose the best beer for your menu with these cool tips.

Pale Ales

- Medium-bodied pale ales balance the flavours of hops and barley. India pale ales tend to be slightly more bitter than regular pale ales. Ales generally have a stronger flavour than traditional beers.

- Pale ales complement lamb, beef roasts and steaks. These beers also go well with rich-tasting poultry, such as turkey and duck. Because they highlight intense flavours, pale ales make a great pairing for spicy dishes.

Lambic beers

- Lambic beers are made from a combination of wheat and malted barley. Fruit is sometimes added during aging. Lambic beers are aged in casks and can be slightly sour when aged for a shorter period, while those varieties that are aged for longer periods tend to be more mellow.

- Because of their fruity flavours, these beers are great alongside fresh fruit dishes. Lambic beers also complement soft-ripened cheeses like brie.

Brown and Amber Ales

- Brown ales are full-bodied, slightly sweet and lightly hopped. The colour is a darker brown or amber colour due to the caramelized malts used to produce these ales. Scotch ale, another form of brown ale, has a strong, malty flavour.

- Brown and amber ales pair with hearty, flavourful foods like Mexican dishes, hamburgers and pizza. Brown ales can also be served with green salads. Amber ales do not make a good match for sweeter foods, because of their malty flavour.

Porters and Stouts

- Porters and stouts are usually heavy, dark and strongly flavoured beers that include roasted malt, which accounts for their dark colour and strong flavour. Most porters have a balanced flavour, both slightly bitter and sweet. Stouts and porters tend to be higher in alcohol content than other varieties of beer.

- The more intense flavours of porters and stouts balance strongly flavoured foods like oysters, smoked cheeses and meat dishes that include brown gravies. Sweeter varieties of stout can also be served with rich, chocolatey desserts.

Lagers and Pilsners

- Lagers tend to be light and bubbly with a golden colour. Pilsners are a light, pale variety of lager—generally with milder flavours and a slightly hoppy taste.

- Lagers' lighter flavours make them a great complement to mild-tasting foods like chicken, fish and green salads. Lagers also work great with fried foods and spicy Asian dishes because of their refreshing qualities.

Bocks

- Though traditionally a German beer, many American varieties of bocks are now available. Bocks tend to be dark and bitter, but they are balanced with some sweetness. Bocks are full-bodied and have a malty flavour.

- Bocks complement hearty grilled fare, including sausages and marinated meats. The strong flavours in bock beers can cut through—and balance out—spicier dishes.

Side by Side

Select any of these sides, alone or in combination, as an accompaniment to your grilling showpiece.

FLAVOUR ACCENTS

Great with any grilled meats or vegetables. (To make butter logs for slicing, see How To, page 84.)

- **Blue Cheese Butter:** Combine 1/4 cup (60 mL) softened butter with 2 tbsp. (30 mL) crumbled Stilton and 1/2 tsp. (2 mL) pepper.

- **Chipotle Butter:** Combine 1/4 cup (60 mL) softened butter with 1 tsp. (5 mL) finely chopped chipotle pepper in adobo sauce.

- **Curry Butter:** Combine 2 tbsp. (30 mL) softened butter, 2 tbsp. (30 mL) olive oil, 2 tsp. (10 mL) hot curry paste and 1 tsp. (5 mL) liquid honey.

- **Peppercorn Rosemary Butter:** Combine 1/4 cup (60 mL) softened butter with 1/2 tsp. (2 mL) crushed black peppercorns and 2 tsp. (10 mL) chopped fresh rosemary.

- **Smoked Paprika Butter:** Combine 1/4 cup (60 mL) softened butter with 2 tsp. (10 mL) smoked sweet paprika.

- **Smoky Cranberry Butter:** Combine 1/4 cup (60 mL) softened butter with 2 tbsp. (30 mL) jellied cranberry sauce and 2 tsp. (10 mL) smoky barbecue sauce.

BREAD

- **French:** Slice a loaf of French bread in half lengthwise. Spread with Peppercorn Rosemary Butter. Wrap in foil. Grill on direct medium heat for about 15 minutes until heated through.

- **Ciabatta:** Cut a loaf of ciabatta or sourdough into 1 inch (2.5 cm) thick slices. Brush both sides with olive oil. Grill on direct medium-low heat for 1 to 2 minutes per side until browned. Spread immediately with mashed roasted garlic. Sprinkle with salt and pepper, or spread with a flavoured butter.

- **Pitas:** Grill Greek-style flat breads on direct medium heat for 1 to 2 minutes per side until warmed through. Brush with Smoked Paprika Butter or your choice of flavoured butter.

VEGETABLES

- **Lettuce:** Cut small heads of romaine lettuce in half lengthwise through stem. Brush all sides with olive oil. Grill on direct medium-high heat until charred along edges. Serve whole with a drizzle of balsamic vinegar or your favourite vinaigrette; or, chop and make into a salad.

- **Corncobs:** Grill corncobs on direct medium-high heat for about 15 minutes until charred and blistered in places. Brush with Smoky Cranberry Butter or your choice of flavoured butter.

- **Vegetable Medley:** Cut a variety of vegetables such as zucchini, eggplant and mushrooms into similar-sized pieces. Toss with melted Curry Butter. Grill on direct medium heat until tender and browned. Brush with more Curry Butter if desired.

POTATOES

- **Baby Fans:** Thinly slice baby potatoes crosswise without cutting through bottom. Put in foil pan. Brush over and between slices with melted Chipotle Butter. Sprinkle with salt and pepper. Cover and seal with foil. Grill on direct medium heat for about 30 minutes until tender.

- **Sweet Potato Packets:** Put 1 lb. (454 g) of thinly sliced, peeled orange-fleshed sweet potato on a sheet of heavy duty or double-layered foil. Drizzle with olive oil. Sprinkle with 1 tsp. (5 mL) of chili powder, and 1/2 tsp. (2 mL) each of cinnamon and grated orange zest. Sprinkle with salt and pepper. Seal packet. Grill on direct medium heat for 10 minutes per side until tender.

- **Blue-Stuffed Potatoes:** Scoop out pulp from 4 medium, cooked potatoes. Mash pulp and combine with 1/2 cup (125 mL) cottage cheese, 2 to 3 tbsp. (30 – 45 mL) Blue Cheese Butter and 1/2 tsp. (2 mL) salt. Fill potatoes and grill on direct medium heat for 20 to 25 minutes until heated through.

FRUIT

Great with chicken, pork or seafood. Or modify with sweet toppings and serve as dessert.

- **Pineapple:** Grill pineapple slices on direct medium-high heat for 2 to 3 minutes per side, brushing with sweet hot mustard or melted Curry Butter, until dark grill marks appear.

- **Peach:** Grill pitted peach halves on direct medium heat for 2 to 3 minutes until dark grill marks appear. Top with little pats of Smoked Paprika Butter or Rosemary Peppercorn Butter.

- **Mango:** Score cross-hatch pattern into mango halves. Rub with jerk seasoning paste and sprinkle with brown sugar and ground allspice. Grill on direct medium-high heat for 1 to 2 minutes until dark grill marks appear.

- **Apple:** Combine equal amounts of butter and maple syrup. Add firm, tart apple wedges and toss. Grill on direct medium heat for 2 to 3 minutes until grill marks appear.

POLENTA

Use prepared polenta roll for convenience.

- Grill 1/2 inch (12 mm) thick slices of polenta on direct medium heat for about 5 minutes per side until heated through and grill marks appear. Top with pats of Blue Cheese Butter or spread with basil pesto.

- Grill 1/2 inch (12 mm) thick slices of polenta on direct medium heat for about 5 minutes per side until grill marks appear. Sprinkle with grated fontina cheese and grill for 1 to 2 minutes more until melted. Spoon prepared bruschetta on top.

- Grill 1/2 inch (12 mm) thick slices of polenta on direct medium heat for about 5 minutes per side until grill marks appear. Spread with olive tapenade and sprinkle with chopped fresh basil.

Index